SEBASTIAN HAFFNER, who was born in Berlin, emigrated to London before the Second World War and returned to Germany in 1954 as the *Observer*'s correspondent there. He has worked as a political columnist for *Die Welt* and *Stern*, and is the author of several books.

GW00480621

THE RISE AND FALL OF
PRUSSIA

Sebastian Haffner

Translated by Ewald Osers

A PHOENIX GIANT PAPERBACK

First published in Great Britain by
George Weidenfeld & Nicolson Ltd in 1980
This paperback edition published in 1998 by Phoenix,
a division of Orion Books Ltd, Orion House,
5 Upper St Martin's Lane, London WC2H 9EA

Translation copyright © Ewald Osers 1980

Originally published in Germany under the title *Preussen ohne Legende*
copyright © Stern Buecher im Verlag Gruner & Jahr

The right of Sebastian Haffner to be identified as the author
of this work has been asserted by him in accordance with
the Copyright, Designs and Patents Act 1988.

A CIP catalogue record for this book is available
from the British Library.

ISBN: 0 75380 143 4

Printed and bound in Great Britain by
Butler & Tanner Ltd, Frome and London

CONTENTS

MAPS

PREFACE

MOST EUROPEAN COUNTRIES can claim a thousand-year-old history – rightly, provided that the contention is not examined too closely.

Not so Prussia. Prussia rose late in the European political sky and went down like a meteor.

After the Migration of Peoples, when the outlines of most of our present European states were beginning to emerge dimly, there was still no hint of any future Prussia. It required a second small migration, the German colonization of the East in the twelfth and thirteenth centuries, for even the prehistory of Prussia to begin.

The prehistory – by no means yet the history. After all, the respectable Ascanian colony on the Spree and Havel rivers and the even more respectable monastic republic of the Knights of the Teutonic Order on the Vistula soon declined again. By the time of the Reformation the state of the Order had become an insignificant Polish territorial appendage, and the Margravate of Brandenburg was still – or again – the poorest and most backward of all German electorates, with a bad reputation as a paradise for robber barons.

No one at that time could have suspected that these two down-at-heel colonies, situated at a great distance from one another, would one day become a brand new European great power. Indeed, it took a good two centuries for this to come about, and, as we shall see, chance played a major part in it. In 1701, when the Elector of Brandenburg called himself King 'in' Prussia, this was still almost a joke.

But from then onwards the development was rapid: half a

century later there was already a King 'of' Prussia, whom his contemporaries called 'the Great'. He challenged three European great powers to war and emerged undefeated from the struggle. The Prussian meteor suddenly stood high in the sky, glittering and sparkling.

Less than half a century later it seemed to fizzle out. But no – there it still was, or there it was again! In 1815 this state, so recently emerged out of nothing and very nearly sunk back into nothingness, was finally established; and alongside Britain, France, Austria and Russia accepted into the exclusive club of the five great European powers, albeit as the smallest of them. In another half a century this state had suddenly become the most important of them all: the King of Prussia was now the German Emperor.

And at that moment of its greatest triumph – no one saw this at the time though anyone can see it now – Prussia began to wither away. It had conquered Germany: now it was being conquered by Germany. The foundation of the German Reich, seen from Prussia's point of view, in spite of all Bismarck's constitutional precautions, proved just a glorious form of abdication.

One may argue about the precise date of Prussia's demise: 1871, when it ceded control of its foreign policy to the new German Reich; 1890, when a public prosecutor from Baden took over the German Foreign Office; 1894, when a Bavarian prince became Prussian Prime Minister; 1918, when the Prussian monarchy was extinguished; 1920, when the Prussian army was absorbed in the Reichswehr; 1932, when a Reich Commissioner deposed the Prussian government; or perhaps only 1945, when flight and expulsion depopulated all but one of the Prussian heartlands.

At that date, at the very latest, Prussia was dead. The Decree of the victorious powers in 1947, which, as an act of supererogation, declared the dissolution of the Prussian state, was no more than the desecration of a corpse.

It would be an exaggeration to say that no one mourned the death of Prussia. On the other hand, one must not confuse mourning for a lost homeland with mourning for the Prussian state – on the contrary, it is remarkable (and admirable) how readily and uncomplainingly people have adjusted to a new citizenship status. But there are in the two present-day German states a great many ex-Prussians – and not only those driven from their homeland – who painfully miss some of the characteristics of their former state: those in the Federal Republic the strict Prussian order and probity, those in the German Democratic Republic the matter-of-fact Prussian liberalism and freedom of thought. However nobody, even by straining their imagination to the utmost, can visualize a possible situation in which Prussia might be resurrected, and no one therefore can desire a rebirth of Prussia in the same earnest way in which many continue to desire a reunification of Germany. Reunification is conceivable, even though unattainable at the moment: a resurrection of Prussia is not. Prussia is dead and the dead cannot be revived.

But we can do something else. We can, now that we have achieved the necessary distance, get a clearer idea of the peculiarity, indeed the uniqueness, of that perished state (which was an artificial creation – one might also say a work of art) than would have been possible in its lifetime. And we can strip its history, which now lies complete before us, of the legends which distorted it while it was still going on: the golden legend according to which the unification of Germany had always been Prussia's mission, a mission deliberately pursued by the Prussian Kings and indeed by the Electors of Brandenburg before them; and also the black legend that refused to see in Prussia anything other than rapacious militarism and branded Frederick the Great and Bismarck as predecessors of Hitler. Both these legends are yesterday's propaganda. The one was the propaganda of the nineteenth-century German Nationalists who wanted to enlist Prussia for their cause; the other, which existed as early as the eighteenth century, was the propaganda of Prussia's neighbours who saw their tranquillity disturbed or even their existence threatened by this uncanny newcomer.

Now that no one has anything more to hope for or to fear from Prussia, the time has come to free ourselves from these outdated misconceptions. Prussia had no German mission: on the contrary, the decline of the German Empire was the condition of Prussia's rise, and when Prussia allowed itself to be persuaded that it had a German mission this became the direct cause of its death. What made eighteenth-century Prussia uncanny, and at times dangerous, to its neighbours was not so much its militarism as its superior quality as a state: its incorruptible administration and independent judiciary, its religious toleration and enlightened education. In its classical period, in the eighteenth century, Prussia quite simply was not only the newest but also the most modern state in Europe. Its crisis began when the French Revolution outstripped it in modernity. From that moment onwards the weaknesses in the Prussian state apparatus began to appear, and there began a search for a new legitimation which finally culminated in a triumphal suicide.

The history of Prussia is an interesting history, even today, or especially today that we know how it ended. It began slowly, developed over a long period, and ended slowly, with a protracted death. But in between lies great drama or, if you like, great tragedy – the tragedy of acting purely for political reasons.

THE SLOW BIRTH

---

*Three Models of Colonization of the East – The Dynastic Policy
of the House of Hohenzollern – The Tragedy of the Great Elector
– How Prussia got its Name*

PRUSSIA'S PREHISTORY is long, several centuries long – much
longer than its history. Where shall we begin? Perhaps the best
starting-point is the name of 'Prussia', a name which underwent
two astonishing changes of meaning.

Originally it was the name of a small heathen Baltic people of
whose origins and history virtually nothing has come down to us;
then, after this unfortunate tribe had been Christianized, with
very brutal methods, by the Order of Teutonic Knights, and in
the course of this process repeatedly decimated, the conquerors
adopted the name of the conquered – a strange and rare event in
history. The state of the Order became known as 'Prussia', and
the German and Slav settlers whom the Order brought into the
country and who gradually mingled with the remainder of the
original Prussians, called themselves Prussians – East Prussians or
West Prussians according to whether they were settled on the
eastern or the western bank of the mouth of the Vistula. As is
well known, East and West Prussia remained the names of the two
extreme north-easterly provinces of the German Reich well into
the twentieth century. Together they constituted Prussia proper.

From 1701 onwards, moreover, a whole state called itself
'Prussia' – a state to which West Prussia did not even belong
initially and for which East Prussia always remained a distant
marginal province; its centre was in a totally different place. This
was the name's second change of meaning: a regional and tribal
name – which, rather confusingly, continued to exist at the same
time – became the name of a state. 'Prussians' from now onwards

were not only just the East Prussians and West Prussians but also the people of Brandenburg and Pomerania, and later of Silesia, as well as of the Rhineland and Westphalia, and gradually, more than two-thirds of all Germans, not to mention the Poles of Posen or the Danes of North Schleswig: in short, all the subjects of the new Hohenzollern state which in 1701 entered the stage as an independent European power and during the next 170 years expanded in all directions in an unsuspected manner.

The name is surprising and calls for an explanation. The Hohenzollerns did not come from Prussia in the geographical sense: they were originally a southern German noble family, and their later residence was not in Königsberg but in Berlin or Potsdam; the heartland of their state never was the original Prussia but invariably the Mark Brandenburg. So why did they call their state Prussia? Why not Brandenburg? They had good reasons and these reasons go far back: they cannot be understood without a knowledge of the Prussian past.

The past, as we have said, is very long, extending over more than half a millennium, and to give a brief outline of it is not easy. But let us attempt it. If we are to succeed we must not lose ourselves in detail but must look upon history the way we do on geological history, dating its periods by geological layers. If we do this we immediately observe three strata.

The oldest – let us call it Prussia's proto-history – is colonial history: the history of the establishment, the flourishing and the decline of two German colonies, the Ascanian colony in Brandenburg and the colony of the Teutonic Order in Prussia. This history begins in the twelfth and thirteenth centuries and ends in the fourteenth and fifteenth, without even a glimmer of a prospect of the future great power of Prussia on the horizon. And yet this colonial history is the primeval soil round Prussia's roots. What was beginning to take shape was not yet the state but the population and social structure characteristic of the later Prussia; and the form it assumed at that primordial period was essentially preserved right into the twentieth century.

The state did not emerge until these two territories came together under one rule. This process of the amalgamation of

'Prussia' and 'Brandenburg' represents the prehistory of Prussia proper – the second, somewhat more recent, layer in the stratification. Again it extends through nearly two centuries, but it is no longer colonial history but dynastic history, the history of princes or, more accurately, the history of one particular princely house, that of Hohenzollern. The Hohenzollerns do not appear in the Mark Brandenburg until the beginning of the fifteenth century or in East Prussia until a whole century later: they therefore have no connection with the earlier colonial history, and their appearance in both territories was originally rather accidental. Nor was it the same branch of the family that was enfeoffed with the Margravate of Brandenburg by the German Emperor in 1415 and with the Duchy of Prussia by the Polish King in 1525. But the Hohenzollerns were a tough and ambitious family with a marked sense of hereditary and dynastic politics, family possessions and family power. By 1618, following a great many political marriages, inheritance treaties and co-enfeoffments, the family possessions became united in one person and the area of dominion doubled. Thus, in a manner of speaking, the embryo of the state to be born eighty-three years later had been begotten.

This period of eighty-three years, the most recent and final layer of Prussian prehistory, may be termed – in contrast to proto- and pre-history – the history of the origin of the Prussian state. It is no longer purely dynastic family or inheritance history, but already political history; its outstanding figure, the 'Great Elector' Frederick Wilhelm, was the first to act, almost in anticipation of what was to come, according to a political creed that was to determine the astonishing actions of the new major state for the next hundred years.

Let us now take a closer look at the three strata. The first and lowest, as we have said, is colonial history – more accurately a section of it, since the history of German colonization of the East in the High Middle Ages also includes territories which never belonged to Prussia, such as Saxony or Mecklenburg, or which came to Prussia very much later, such as Holstein. But the four heartlands of what was to be Prussia later – Brandenburg, Pomerania, Silesia, and 'Prussia' proper – are sufficient to illustrate the

7

variety of processes that are summed up under the heading of 'German colonization of the East', as well as their different results. Colonization is always aggression, the conquest of weaker nations and civilizations by stronger ones. It is also always progress, just because a weaker and more primitive civilization gives way to a stronger and higher one. It is therefore always a mixture of good and bad, and one's judgement has to depend on whether the good outweighs the bad.

The best solution, of course, is the achievement of progress without colonization – when a nation adopts a higher alien civilization upon its own initiative, the way Japan did in recent history. That kind of thing also occurred in medieval Europe. The 'Japan' of that early period of colonization was Poland, which had been a Christian kingdom through its own efforts since the tenth century, almost as long as Germany. Bohemia and Hungary, the lands of the slightly younger Crowns of St Wenceslas and St Stephen, also avoided colonization by accepting Christianity and the higher Christian civilization. It was against this East-European barrier that, in a sense, the wave of German colonization – which of course always sailed under the flag of Christianization – was broken. There was nothing left for it to achieve there. Its objects (and also its victims) were the smaller, weaker, more 'underdeveloped' (i.e. pagan) tribes between Germany and Poland. To them, in the twelfth and thirteenth centuries, German monks, knights and peasants brought Christianity and 'culture' – together with subjection and alien rule. These things never happened without bloodshed. But there were considerable differences in degree. We can clearly distinguish three models.

Christianization and colonization were mildest in Pomerania and Silesia – regions which had been 'licked by Christianity' even before the advent of the Germans. Their Slav tribal rulers (in Silesia often the scions of Polish families) were often already Christians who ruled pagan subjects and who, to consolidate their rule, called in German monks and settlers as in a sense development aid officials. It cannot be denied that these Germans provided very effective development aid. Nor can it be denied that development aid frequently turned into land seizure, and peaceful mission into forcible baptism; and that many more arrived than had been invited, and even more followed. Naturally, this gave rise to quarrels and bloodshed, but there never was anything like a real military conquest of Silesia or Pomerania; the Germanization of these countries proceeded gradually through the peaceful intermingling of new arrivals and natives. Nor should one picture an invading German land-owning aristocracy imposing itself simply as an upper class upon the indigenous Slav peasantry – as happened, for instance, in the Baltic lands, Kurland, Livland (Livonia) and Estonia. In Pomerania and Silesia there was intermingling at all levels of the feudal social pyramid, from the princely families through the landed gentry down to the peasants. This process took place throughout several centuries. Gradually the German language and the superior Christian civilization the Germans had brought with them prevailed – but the snub noses of the Junker families and the many aristocratic names ending in the Slav 'ow' and 'itz' to this day testify to the Slav origin even of the ruling classes. There was no question of extermination, nor even of real subjection of the natives; it was far more a case of infiltration which imperceptibly changed into absorption.

The colonial history of the Mark Brandenburg was a good deal rougher. Although Albrecht the Bear, the founder of the Ascanian dynasty which colonized the Mark in the twelfth century, had acquired a corner of that territory legally, as the appointed heir of a Wendish prince who had been converted to Christianity, he had the major part of it given to himself as a feoff by the Emperor (pagan lands were regarded as not having rulers) and thereafter conquered it in regular campaigns. His conquest was followed for decades to come by rebellions and suppression: a bloody history, not a pleasant one. Besides, the intermingling of the German settlers with the Wendish natives, which followed conquest in Brandenburg, was never quite as complete as it was further east: very much later, in the eighteenth and nineteenth centuries, Wends in the Mark were still, either voluntarily or involuntarily, living among their own kind, in their suburbs on the fringe of towns; in the Spreewald, the then almost inaccessible

9

woodlands along the Spree, a small Wendish ethnic group, with its own language and customs, survives to the present day.

On the other hand, after conquest and colonization, Brandenburg became an important country with its own characteristics very much faster than Pomerania or Silesia – these two continued to live in the shadows for a long time as much subdivided small principalities. The Margraves of Brandenburg, by way of contrast, soon rose to the top rank of the German Empire's nobility: as early as the thirteenth century, in the role of 'Reich Chamberlains', they belonged to the exclusive club of Electors who elected the German Emperor, and during the heyday of the Ascanians Brandenburg was a power in the Empire. That power declined when the dynasty died out; its new aristocracy reverted to nature, and the Mark, under a succession of dynasties, became a kind of 'Wild East', where robber barons flourished and the only law was the law of the stronger. This need not concern us any further. We merely wanted to point out that the colonial history of the Mark took a course different from that of Pomerania and Silesia, surpassing it both in good and evil. On the one hand it was more violent and bloody, on the other it was politically more fruitful and creative. Albrecht the Bear was a brutal conqueror, but the Mark Brandenburg of the Ascanians, before its decline, was a viable and vital state. In a sense all colonial history has these two aspects to it, with greater or lesser contrast.

Much more even than in Brandenburg this contrast was apparent in the original Prussia – the territory we must now consider in somewhat greater detail. The conquest and subjection of the Prussian lands on the Vistula by the Order of the Teutonic Knights is a tale of atrocities; yet the state which the Order established on the territory thus conquered was a small miracle of its day. And the decline and fall of this early proto-Prussia led directly to the emergence of the great power called Prussia.

The beginnings of its colonization are marked by a decade of horrible massacre, almost extermination, comparable to the later near-extermination of the North American Indians by the European immigrants. No attempt will be made to whitewash it. But the horrors of that history may be explained by two things:

the crusading spirit of the conquerors and the enormous civilization gap between them and their victims. Let us start with the latter.

The pagan Slavs on the Elbe and Oder at the time of their colonization undoubtedly lagged far behind their Christian colonizers in their material, cultural and religious civilization – though not that far behind that they may not have been susceptible to assimilation or development. The pagan Prussians on the lower Vistula, on the other hand, were, in German (and indeed also in Polish) eyes, not backward kinsmen but savages: a people of different race, without writing and without calendar, with a language equally incomprehensible to Germans and Slavs, and with customs that seemed barbarian to their Christian neighbours, such as polygamy and the exposure of unwanted children; yet at the same time warlike, tough and courageous. If the Christian neighbours were to appear in Prussia as missionaries or colonizers, as the Poles had tried to do unsuccessfully before the Teutonic Knights, then the clash could only be frightful.

It would be doubly frightful if the missionaries and colonizers happened to have recently returned from the Crusades with the slogan of 'Death to the Infidels!'. In Brandenburg conquest and mission had been two different things: the temporal conquerors had demanded only submission; the Christian mission work was done by peaceful monks who, moreover, brought with them many a useful technology. The Cistercian Order, for instance, the principal missionaries in the Mark, were experts in the drainage of marshes. In Prussia, on the other hand, the conquering Knights of the Order brought Christianity by the sword. Baptism was their first and principal demand from the perplexed Prussians: anyone refusing it was put to death. To the Prussians this invasion was a frightful experience of violation. Total strangers, armed to the teeth, burst into the country for no reason at all and, in an incomprehensible language, were demanding incomprehensible things and killing unless promptly obeyed.

This went on for ten years, from 1226 to 1236, followed by a period of peace: the peace of the graveyard. And then suddenly in 1260 the great Prussian rebellion erupted, spreading through the entire land like wildfire – an act of desperation by the primitive Prussians which, given their inadequate political organization, seems almost beyond comprehension. At first the rebellion was victorious, with horrible deeds of revenge no less atrocious than the actions of the conquerors. In the long run, of course, the superior military civilization of the Knights of the Order prevailed; even so, a small-scale war raged on for fifteen years, becoming more and more a war of extermination. It is a miracle that any Prussians survived after it ended.

But some did survive. Contrary to widespread belief the Prussians were not totally exterminated, but their remnants became so thoroughly intermixed during the next few centuries with the colonist population now brought into the country – no doubt not entirely without some forcible encouragement – that virtually nothing has survived of their language or history. Incidentally, this colonist population so vigorously promoted by the Order consisted not only of Germans but also of Christian Slavs from the neighbourhood – Kashubians, Masurians, Masovians and indeed also Poles. The Order was not fussy: itself sterile, in accordance with the monastic rule, it needed a neo-Prussian Christian people and created it.

Frightful as the Order was as a conqueror, its subsequent colonizing and state-creating achievement was admirable. The horrors of the thirteenth century were followed in the fourteenth by a period when the Order blossomed like a rose. Its origin is the most atrocious chapter in German colonial history; but what was created with such carnage now became a model colony. This sort of thing happens time and again in history: horrible deeds are done; and then new people arrive on the scene and are active and cheerful on the graves.

The fourteenth-century organization of the Order strikes one as strangely modern: here, in the midst of feudal monarchies, was a monastic republic headed by an elected Grand Master, surrounded by his Chapter, just as a present-day head of state or government might be by his ministers. The country was divided into twenty districts, each of them governed, in accordance with the Grand Master's directives, by a Comptroller with his own

Convention – all of them Knights of the Order, in a sense civil servants. No feudal lords as elsewhere – the rule of the Order prohibited personal property, and besides they were all unmarried since their vows demanded chastity. Their ranks were replenished from the Empire, where the Grand Master continually recruited without much difficulty. Soon the Order, according to contemporary witnesses, became a 'Hospital', with opportunities for a brilliant career for the younger sons of the German princely families eager for high office. It was in a position to choose the best and for a long time was exceedingly well governed.

That, then, was the state, and this state created for itself a people – a people of immigrants who, upon arrival, found a ready-made state and a ready-made administration, and had their land assigned to them: fertile land, almost empty after the fighting, a land of unlimited opportunity for those who worked hard and efficiently. And they were hard-working and efficient, those immigrants. Prussia grew rich in the fourteenth century, far richer than the other German colonies, with cities growing rapidly, such as Danzig and Königsberg, with an efficiently working aristocracy (a purely economic aristocracy since politics were the preserve of the Order) and a peasantry far freer and more prosperous than in the neighbouring feudal territories. A fortunate country.

No, not a fortunate country. The more the 'estates' prospered, the more they felt domination by the Order to be alien rule – which, of course, it was and in a sense remained. After all, the Order was deliberately replenishing its ranks from the Empire and not from the local aristocracy or patricians. These now cast envious glances at nearby Poland, where the nobility was growing increasingly powerful and the kingdom was rapidly turning into a republic of nobles. Thus, when in the fifteenth century the Order found itself involved in a long series of wars with Poland and Lithuania, it found its 'estates' – its people – at first partly and eventually totally on the enemy side. That was what wrecked the state of the Order – that and presumably also a certain gradual degeneration and reversion to nature. Poverty, chastity and obedience do not in the long run stand up to the temptations of power.

In this rapid survey we are being deliberately sparing with names and dates. We did not mention the famous Grand Masters Hermann von Salza, Winrich von Kniprode or Heinrich von Plauen, and we would even prefer not to mention the famous battle of Tannenberg (1410), the first heavy defeat of the Order, in a sense the Battle of the Marne of its Polish wars. It has gone down in the German and Polish historical legend as a subject of heroic lament on the one side and jubilation over liberation on the other – but it decided nothing yet. The wars between the Order and Poland continued after Tannenberg for more than half a century. One date, however, is indispensable, both to the history of the Order and to the prehistory of Prussia: 1466, the year of the Second Peace of Thorn. As a result the Order lost its independence to Poland. West Prussia became totally Polish (and during the next few centuries was permeated by Polish settlers who never left again). East Prussia was left to the Order, but only as a Polish feoff. That was a major break in history.

Subsequent German national historiography assessed it as a national disaster. Yet no one saw it as that at the time. The fifteenth century did not think in terms of nationality, and many of the German subjects of the Order regarded transition to the much looser Polish feudal domination as liberation. Emperor and Empire did not stir a finger. Yet the transition of East Prussia into Polish feudal sovereignty provided the first prerequisite for the subsequent emergence on its soil of a new sovereign state: henceforward Prussia was no longer a part of the Empire. Centuries were to pass before it detached itself again from Poland – but the very first secret step towards the emergence of the future Prussian state had been taken.

The second followed in 1525, when the last Grand Master used the Reformation for dissolving the state of the Teutonic Order and making himself a temporal 'Duke of Prussia' – still, of course, under Polish feudal supremacy. This is a somewhat unsavoury story, as are so many princely stories of the age of the Reformation: as is well known, the princes frequently turned the Reformation into a business proposition in which the gospels had to provide the pretext for the grabbing of ecclesiastical property. In the case of the last Grand Master there was additionally the betrayal of his office and those who had elected him to that office; he was therefore proscribed by the Empire but this did not worry him greatly. He continued to reign, proscribed but unchallenged, for several decades – and not so badly either (he was the founder of Königsberg University). He got married like any other temporal ruler and left his Duchy to a feeble-minded son. This faintly unsavoury story of the treacherous last Grand Master and first Duke of Prussia would not be worth mentioning had he not been a member of a very particular family. He was a Hohenzollern, Albrecht von Brandenburg-Ansbach, and it was through him that East Prussia was brought into the same family as Brandenburg. It was only natural that this family should now make every possible effort to unite the Margravate and the Duchy in the same person.

This brings us into the second geological layer of the Prussian past, the one that is no longer colonial history but dynastic history, the history of the domestic politics of the House of Hohenzollern. Later, when the Hohenzollerns had become Prussian kings and German emperors, this period was glorified beyond its deserts, just as though the electors of Brandenburg in the fifteenth and sixteenth centuries had all been deliberately working towards the future greatness of Prussia or indeed Germany. They did nothing of the kind – none of them. They were average German territorial princes, no better and no worse than many who are now forgotten, and they pursued the same busy and petty family politics as the rest of them: a policy of marriage and inheritance aimed at the acquisition of 'claims' and the gathering into family ownership of as many territories as possible. Otherwise they were in perpetual opposition to the gradually weakening central imperial power and, simultaneously, constantly squabbling with their own 'estates' – nobility, clergy and cities – which opposed the central powers of the princes in exactly the same way as the princes opposed those of the emperor. These speculations and squabbles, now utterly boring, filled two centuries. An entire century was to pass before the Mark Hohenzollerns had more or less tamed their domestic robber barons, and another before their 'claims' began to bear fruit.

The Hohenzollerns, originally a Swabian family, had come to Franconia at the end of the twelfth century and for the next 200 years were Burgraves of Nuremberg, a titular dignity rather than a genuine position of rule. At the same time they acquired small territorial domains in and around Ansbach and Bayreuth. During these 200 years they prospered more as officers of the Empire than as territorial princes. The sixth Burgrave of Nuremberg, for example, who subsequently (1415) became the first Hohenzollern Margrave of Brandenberg, had made his career as the adviser and agent of the Emperor Sigismund whom, by his diplomatic skill, he had helped to get elected to the imperial throne; the Margravate of Brandenburg was his reward. A truly imperial reward and a considerable promotion – but also a burden which the rewarded and promoted Margrave was to find exceedingly tedious. He soon left the Mark again, discouraged by annoying and rather unprofitable struggles against its degenerate nobility. His son, similarly, could not bear to remain there, and the third Hohenzollern Margrave hardly ever visited his country. The business and squabbles of the Empire continued for some time to be more interesting to this Swabian-Franconian family of politicians than their new territorial dominion in the remote 'sand-box of the Empire'. Only in the fourth generation did the Hohenzollerns strike root there and reign as fathers of their people, no better and no worse than other princes; still interested to an equal if not greater measure in establishing inheritance claims elsewhere, in the western Empire as well as in Pomerania, and indeed also in Silesia – claims which, though carefully nurtured, did not come to anything for a long time. And then, suddenly, chance tossed the biggest of them, the Prussian one, into their lap.

It was the purest chance that the last Grand Master of the Order, who had reformed and secularized the state, was a Hohenzollern; until then the Hohenzollerns had not had anything to do with the Order at all. It was not even as though the Hohenzollern ruler of Brandenburg at the time, Joachim I, had pulled any strings in connection with his kinsman's Prussian transaction which suddenly opened up such surprising prospects to the family. On the contrary, Joachim I was an inveterate opponent of the Reformation and a close ally of his brother, the Archbishop of Magdeburg and Mainz, a notorious dealer in indulgences. He profoundly disapproved of what his cousin was doing in Prussia, and it was not until after the death of the Margrave of Brandenburg that the Hohenzollerns seized their unexpected chance in Prussia. Then, admittedly, they did so thoroughly. Joachim II not only introduced the Reformation in Brandenburg as well, against his real religious convictions, but with a great deal of trouble and many concessions at the time of the death of the old Prussian Albrecht, in 1568, he achieved his own co-enfeoffment with the Prussian inheritance from the Polish king and moreover – to make assurance doubly sure – married two of his sons to the daughters of the 'idiot' Albrecht Frederick, the new Duke of Prussia. This Duke, however, against all expectations, lived for a very long time, 'reigning' for another fifty years. Only Joachim II's great-grandson eventually came into the inheritance, and in 1618 Brandenburg and Prussia were at last united in the hands of the same Hohenzollern ruler.

We are skipping through all this very briefly because the details of this princely dynastic policy are really of no interest to the present-day reader. But one should not forget the snail-like slowness with which it all actually happened. 1415 – the Hohenzollerns in Brandenburg; 1466 – Prussia under Polish sovereignty; 1525 – a Hohenzollern, now a Polish vassal, is Duke of Prussia; 1568 – co-enfeoffment of the Brandenburg Hohenzollerns; 1618 – the inheritance. It sounds like a rapid development and in retrospect looks like a series of preplanned staging posts along a predetermined road leading straight to the Prussian Hohenzollern state. But in fact it took centuries, and between every two stages entire generations lived and died without any suspicion of what the next stage would be or whether there would be another one

at all, or how it would all continue. In fact, it might have continued quite differently at every stage. The subsequent myth of
the House of Hohenzollern represented events as though that
House, in co-operation with Providence, had been consciously
and far-sightedly working towards the future Prussia, 'laying
its foundations'. Even in our century schoolchildren used to
memorize the destinies of the Teutonic Order and the reigns
of the Electors of Brandenburg with as much reverence as if they
were the Old and the New Testament of their country. In actual
fact the fifteenth- and sixteenth-century Electors of Brandenburg – not to mention the thirteenth- and fourteenth-century
Knights of the Teutonic Order – would all have been exceedingly
surprised to learn that they were blazing the trail of some future
Prussia. A great deal of chance was needed even for a Brandenburg Elector to become also Duke of Prussia. The accidental,
arbitrary and somehow not quite convincing nature of its origins
became attached to the Prussian state throughout its history as
if it were some curse, some present put in its cradle by a wicked
fairy. In a sense Prussia need not have come into being, it was
not indispensable. Europe was at all times entirely conceivable
without Prussia – unlike any other European state – and throughout its existence Prussia always required an excess of political will
to live and military self-assertion to compensate for that congenital
flaw.

Frederick the Great, who was no creator of myths – indeed, if
anything, an exploder of myths – wrote in his *Memorabilia of the
House of Brandenburg* that the history of the House really only
began to become interesting with the electorship of Johann
Sigismund. Not, by any means, because of the personality of
that Elector. He was no remarkable ruler. He only reigned for
eleven years, from 1608 to 1619, prematurely wrecked his health
by gluttony and drunkenness, and had virtually been incapable
of government for a number of years when he died at the age of
forty-seven. But it was under that pleasure-seeking baroque prince
that two great inheritance claims came to fruition which enor-
mously increased his dominions and lent them prospects for the

future: in 1609 that of Jülich-Cleves in the west, which remained controversial for a long time to come and abruptly involved Brandenburg in the politics of the western great powers France and Holland; and in 1618 the above-mentioned Prussian inheritance in the east which drew Brandenburg into the Swedish-Polish field of force and conflict – a tremendous territorial accretion but one encumbered with entirely new political demands and dangers. It might be said that these inheritances imposed greatness upon the House of Hohenzollern, a constraint that was to become the law governing the life of the state of Prussia.

The first to realize this was Johann Sigismund's grandson. His son, a particularly weak and timid ruler, was plagued by entirely different constraints: 1618, the year of personal union between Brandenburg and Prussia, was also the beginning of the Thirty Years' War, during which Brandenburg was so thoroughly devastated that one would have been justified in doubting that it would ever recover. It was devastated both by the Swedes and by the Imperials, between whom the Elector helplessly fluctuated, and eventually even by his own troops whom he had hired in extreme distress but whom he had not been able to pay. Unable to expel the foreign armies they turned into a third plague. But faraway Prussia was more or less spared by the war and in the post-war period became the temporary centre of the Hohenzollern lands and the basis of their reconstruction. Moreover, the Peace Treaty of Westphalia eventually made the Hohenzollerns, in spite of what their lands had suffered, war profiteers in two respects: first, the collapse of imperial power made them, together with all other princelings, virtually sovereign in the Empire (though not in Prussia which remained under Polish sovereignty), and second, there were new and important territorial gains: in the east Eastern Pomerania and Cammin, in the west the lands of the former Bishoprics of Minden and Halberstadt and a claim to the Archbishopric of Magdeburg.

The dynastic power of the Hohenzollerns was considerable after 1648, in the same class as that of the houses of Wittelsbach, Wettin or Guelph, though not yet that of the Habsburgs. But it was based on five geographically disjointed chunks of territory, two big ones and three lesser ones; Magdeburg alone bordered on Brandenburg. Whenever the ruler wished to travel from one of his domains to another he had to pass through foreign territory. In addition, his countries did not constitute a uniform political unit but were seven or eight separate dominions linked merely by personal union. Their lord did not wear a crown but a good half-dozen hats: he was Margrave of Brandenburg, Duke of Prussia, Pomerania, Magdeburg and Cleves, Count of the (Rhenish) Mark, Prince of Minden, Prince of Halberstadt. Each of his principalities had its own institutions and laws – its own constitution, as it were – in each of them the ruler encountered different domestic oppositions and restrictions upon his sovereign powers, and each of them wished to be ruled in the ancient way by its own 'estates'.

The task facing a prince in such a situation was obvious. He had to try to link up his geographically dispersed domains by somehow acquiring or conquering the territories separating them; and he had to transform individual domains with their own characteristics into a unified state. Indeed each of these was the prerequisite of the other, since without a unified state the external strength for an expansionist territorial policy would be lacking, and without successful territorial rounding off the internal strength for checking the divergent special interests would not exist. A Herculean and really unrealizable double task!

The man who tackled it and throughout a reign of almost fifty years wrestled with it ceaselessly has gone down in history by the name of 'the Great Elector' – and he deserves this title of honour: his life and work had greatness. But to go further and credit him with being the real founder of Prussia is an exaggeration. For what the Great Elector actually achieved in a long life of enormous heroic endeavour was very little; in fact only one thing: the sovereignty of Prussia (East Prussia) by the liberation of that country from Polish supremacy (1660). Admittedly this achievement, fought for and won in a prolonged and bloody Swedish-Polish war, after two changes of alliance, proved to have exceptionally important consequences under his successor.

In every other respect the reign of the Great Elector Frederick Wilhelm, a record of virtually ceaseless war at home and abroad, is strangely unproductive. It is reminiscent of the sufferings of Sisyphus or of Tantalus – time and again the heavy stone pushed up the mountainside will roll down again, time and again the desperately coveted and almost grasped drink is snatched away from the lips at the last moment. Western Pomerania, for example, the urgently needed link between Brandenburg and Eastern Pomerania-Cammin, was twice conquered by the Elector and had twice to be surrendered again. Other territorial endeavours had similar outcomes. At his death in 1688 the territory of the Great Elector was virtually the same as it had been forty years earlier, and that in spite of perpetual wars, campaigns, battles won and lost, acts of heroic bravura, and enough risky switching of alliances to make anyone giddy.

To posterity the Great Elector presents himself in the apotheosis of Andreas Schlüter, whose equestrian statue stood for two and half centuries on the *Lange Brücke* in what is now East Berlin and which today stands in front of West Berlin's Charlottenburg Castle: as a triumphant Roman *Imperator* he rides proudly over his defeated enemies who, in chains and in impotent anger, adorn the plinth of his monument. Schlüter's statue is a superb work of art but in terms of history it is false to the point of being ludicrous. Never in his life had Frederick Wilhelm been triumphant; invariably he himself had been the one in chains, the one in impotent rebellion; his greatness resides in the fact that his rebellion never ceased. His enemies or allies (his continuous switching of alliances was, as we have said, enough to make you giddy) were invariably stronger than he: France and Holland and at times also the Emperor, in the west; and Sweden and Poland in the east. That he was even a participant and an actor in their great game, and moreover continuously, and continuously changing sides between powers able to crush him – that had something astonishing about it, something magnificent, a boldness or indeed an impressive impertinence. Admittedly this impertinence was prompted – or, if you like, dictated – by statecraft; but this was the statecraft of a state not yet properly in being, a state yet to be created by the gamble of the Great Elector's policy.

Friedrich Wilhelm was a visionary. Not only did he engage in great power politics without a basis of real power but he also built up a small fleet and acquired an African colony. He wanted to be the equal not only of the great continental powers but also of the new naval powers. His realistic grandson, who was to become the true architect of the Prussian state, sold it all off again. The end result of Frederick Wilhelm's military and grandly conceived – one might say, maliciously, megalomaniac – foreign policy was virtually nothing; it was enough of a miracle, and indeed of an accomplishment, that it all came off without disaster. It was after the Brandenburg victory at Fehrbellin (1675) over the Swedes, who then had the reputation of being the best soldiers in Europe, that the term 'the Great Elector' came into use in the courts of Europe and in the press for the Brandenburger, reflecting respect but also a touch of sarcasm; after all, an elector was nothing great, and to speak of a 'Great Elector' was somewhat like speaking of a 'great dwarf'. That is precisely what he was all his life.

Not only in foreign affairs but also at home. The Great Elector made tremendous efforts to transform his disparate territories into one state, but in domestic affairs also his achievement was only one: a small regular army (initially 6,000 and eventually 28,000 men), together with the fiscal authority he needed for paying them. But at what cost! The Brandenburg Diet decision of 1653 made the Junkers petty kings on their estates, with their own judiciary and police powers, and things were even worse elsewhere. When we referred to the Great Elector as a man in chains we were thinking above all of the restraints imposed on him everywhere by his 'estates' – principally the landed gentry – which, throughout his life, he tried to break as Gulliver did the bonds of the Lilliputians.

This struggle never ceased. The most recalcitrant nobles were those of East Prussia, long accustomed to conspiring against their territorial ruler with their envied Polish peers. In 1679 – near the end of his life and reign – the Elector had one of them, a Colonel von Kalkstein, picked up in Warsaw, taken to Prussia and beheaded at Memel: a deed testifying not so much to the dominance of a tyrant as to the desperation of a man perpetually frustrated. His successors, incidentally, never won the struggle of kingship against the nobility either. Eventually they arrived at a *modus vivendi*, and Prussia always remained a state of Junkers. We shall deal with this aspect later. Similarly we shall save for a later chapter the Great Elector's immigration policy which marked the beginning of a long-term Prussian tradition.

In short, he did not succeed in establishing Prussia, in establishing the Brandenburg-Prussian great power – although, without any doubt, he was the first to have that vision of a future state clearly before him. He was a Moses allowed to see the Promised Land but not to enter it. His Herculean efforts to create power from impotence ultimately remained unsuccessful: that was his tragedy. His son and heir went about it differently.

This son and heir, Frederick, the first Prussian king, has had a raw deal from Prussian-German historians – perhaps a little too raw. At times one has the impression that they found it positively embarrassing to have to depict such an unheroic king as the creator and first bearer of the Prussian crown. But he possessed other good qualities for a ruler – qualities which nowadays are esteemed even more highly than the heroic ones. He was an educated man and maintained an educated court – something for which his rough colonial territories had not been remarkable in the past. The fact that his capital, though perhaps initially with a slight touch of irony, acquired the label of 'the Athens on the Spree' is due to him. He adorned Berlin with its first famous buildings – the Palace, the Armoury, Charlottenburg Castle – founded the Academy of Arts and the Academy (originally Society) of Sciences, he was a patron of Schlüter; and the Queen, an intellectual, was a patron of Leibniz. Of course Frederick was a spendthrift. His son and heir who, when he became king, did everything quite differently from his father, described his court as 'the craziest household in the world'. But Frederick's crazy household did produce something tangible; his extravagance was not entirely ignoble.

All this is incidental. Our subject is not the Hohenzollern kings but the state of Prussia, and Frederick I's generous support of culture interests us only to the extent that it, too, initiated a Prussian tradition – one that is often overlooked. Frederick's real major achievement was, of course, the acquisition of the royal title. This was accomplished peacefully and without violence or military glory, through many years of patient and painstaking diplomatic negotiation. Maybe that is why it plays such a modest – one is almost tempted to say shamefaced – role in Prussian historical myth which, as we all know, is so fond of the sound of trumpets. None the less, this was the decisive step towards the goal the Great Elector had all his life striven and made heroic efforts for, and failed to achieve: the transformation of a collection of small and medium-sized principalities into one state.

Frederick the Great, who did not have a single good word to say about his grandfather, ascribed his royal title to nothing but vanity: from sheer vanity he had desired and acquired an empty dignity, grasped the semblance of power without a real power base. That, with respect, is a superficial judgement. Appearance, in politics, is itself a part of power – as Frederick the Great knew perfectly well himself and indeed on occasions stated. The halo of invincibility frequently prevents wars and battles, and anyone governing people by appealing to their imagination needs less violence to rule them. The royal title, about 1700, was a magic word (much as the word 'democracy' is today). To have grasped this instinctively is what sets Frederick I above his father. It was a brainwave. Not everyone had it.

Of course, it had been in the air ever since the Treaty of Westphalia. That peace treaty had destroyed the power of the Emperor; the great German princes now all felt like kings and were anxious to call themselves kings. On the other hand, they still shrank from making themselves kings directly within their Empire territories. A king of Brandenburg – that would have sounded like a provocation: after all, Emperor and Empire still existed; even so Kings of Bavaria, Saxony and Württemberg were still unthinkable about 1700, and when they actually emerged a century later, in Napoleonic times, that signalled the end of the Empire. That moment had not yet come in 1700 – but a few of the great princely houses found a way out: they acquired foreign royal crowns. The Wettins of Saxony in 1697 became Kings of Poland and thereby, tacitly, were kings also in Saxony; the Guelphs of Hanover in 1715 became Kings of England – and hence also kings in Hanover. It is interesting, as a historical curiosity, that half a century earlier the Hohenzollerns had had a similar opportunity. After the death of Gustavus Adolphus there had been a project to marry the heiress to his throne, who later became Queen Christina, to the heir to the throne of Brandenburg, later the Great Elector. If that had come off the Hohenzollerns would have become not Kings of Prussia but Kings of Sweden and would have ruled over a compact Swedish-German Baltic realm; God knows what would have happened then. However, it did not come off, mainly because of Christina's stubborn dislike of marriage; as is well known, she never married at all, later became a Catholic and was altogether odd. Under the Elector Frederick no foreign throne was waiting for the Hohenzollerns. But did they not themselves possess a foreign land? Suddenly – one only had to think of it – it was a valuable fact that Prussia, East Prussia, since time immemorial, since 1466, had not belonged to the Empire but had for several centuries been under Polish sovereignty, and that the Great Elector had succeeded in freeing himself from that suzerainty – his only foreign policy success. In Prussia Frederick was not just a prince of the Empire but a sovereign, and there he could quite legitimately become King, just as the Saxons in Poland or the Hanoverians in England. Admittedly only 'in' Prussia. That was a point to which Poland in particular attached importance – since, after all, it still possessed the other part of Prussia, West Prussia. On no account did Poland wish to sanction a claim to West Prussia.

The negotiations which preceded recognition of the new royal title, mainly with the Emperor and the King of Poland, were tricky and difficult. The greatest difficulty – another historical curiosity – was raised by the Teutonic Order. Yes, it actually still existed. Even though it had lost its Prussian land (amidst noisy protestations) in 1525, its German organization, its foreign recruiting office, had survived (Napoleon was to dissolve the Order in 1809). Staunchly Catholic, the Order had meanwhile closely allied itself to the House of Habsburg (the 'Hoch- und Deutschmeister' march, 'We are the Royal-Imperial Infantry Regiment', is to this day one of the most famous marches of the Austrian Army), and in Vienna therefore it mobilized its entire influence to prevent that heretical, illegitimate, stolen Prussian Duchy of the Hohenzollerns from becoming recognized as a kingdom. As we know, their efforts were in vain. On 18 January 1701 the Elector Frederick III of Brandenburg placed the crown upon his head in Königsberg and henceforward was Frederick I, King 'in' Prussia.

That 'in', of course, was a blemish, but it applied only to the outside world – a concession which the electoral negotiators had been forced to make for the sake of recognition. Internally Frederick was right from the start the unchallenged first King 'of' Prussia – no longer, as in the past, a Margrave in one place, a Duke in another, and a Count or a Prince elsewhere. All his lands now constituted the kingdom of 'Prussia', even though the people of Brandenburg, the Rhineland or Westphalia would never have dreamt that all of a sudden they would be bearing the name of that far-away eastern land. From now on they were all Prussian subjects, governed by royal Prussian officials, garrisoned by a royal Prussian army and – such is human nature – soon no longer grumbling but indeed proud of belonging to a great, respected and feared state. Their local and regional loyalties had suffered a decisive blow. Frederick had made one important conquest: as King of Prussia he had seized the imagination of his subjects. And that alone was what enabled his son to achieve what his father had failed to achieve – to transform scattered domains into a genuine well-functioning state. That task still lay ahead.

Prussia was still just a programme. But that programme had now been proclaimed and at home largely accepted. Prussia's long gestation had run its course. It had emerged and its history was about to begin.

THE RUGGED RATIONAL STATE

The Two Great Kings – A Military Revolution – Kingship and Junkerdom – The Three Prussian Indifferences

THE 'PRUSSIAN PROGRAMME', a programme of political consolidation and expansion, proclaimed in 1701, was carried out in the eighteenth century with a punctuality and completeness that amazed the contemporaries. Indeed it may be said that the two kings of Prussia under whose reigns this was done both surpassed their targets: Frederick Wilhelm I, 'our greatest internal king', transformed the collection of territories he had inherited not merely into a state but into the most disciplined, most modern and most efficient military state of his day; his son Frederick, called by his contemporaries 'the Great' (a title which posterity should not pettishly withhold), gave that state not only, at long last, a coherent territorial shape, which it had so patently lacked until then, but simultaneously made it into a great European power.

The achievements of both these Prussian kings were exceptional, not only in historical retrospect but in the eyes of their marvelling contemporaries. However, one would be missing the point if one were to regard eighteenth-century classical Prussia, which suddenly emerged into life from nothingness and then spread on the map like a patch of oil, simply as the personal achievement of these two kings. The spirit of the age was a factor in the development – the spirit of political reason, of statecraft, which became dominant throughout Europe at that time and which favoured such an artificial rational state as Prussia, and indeed called for such a model state. Prussia was being blown forward by a powerful wind. It was not only new, it was modern – one might also say, it was smart.

There was one other contributory factor, perhaps even a decisive factor. Sheer necessity, the urge for self-preservation, inborn in any state organism as it is in an individual, which in the case of such an unorganic, accidentally assembled, structure – as the Kingdom of Prussia proclaimed in 1701 still was – simply demanded rounding off and territorial expansion, i.e. conquest, and this in turn required the utmost tightening and concentration of forces internally.

The Great Elector had failed because he had tried to do both things at once; his grandson and great-grandson succeeded because they shared the two tasks in a manner demanded by reason – by statecraft. Territorial expansion, necessary as it was if the state was to endure, demanded power, and that power had first to be *created*. This was done by Frederick Wilhelm I, the 'soldier king'. Frederick the Great then *applied* that power, and at the same time gambled with it : he was lucky, his great gamble came off.

Neither father nor son acted from any personal motive, from the creative arbitrariness of genius realizing a personal vision. Instead they both acted in response to the hard constraints of circumstances, constraints which must have been felt also by their collaborators and indeed by many of their subjects; otherwise resistance would have been much greater and success would have been far less striking. Of course, in the case of Prussia, more than in any other, one must be careful to avoid myths of historical inevitability or predestination – there never was any historical predestination about that state : its constituent parts had been brought together by accident, it had not grown but it had been made. But that it had to be made unless that product of chance was to fall apart again, that it had to expand in order merely to survive – that was so patent, to the king as much as to the simplest subject, that it was unchallengeable. And in this sense it is possible, without indulging in political myths, to say that the 'Prussian idea', the 'Prussian programme', was exercising some intangible impersonal power (or constituted such a power) that forced kings and subjects alike into its service.

Indeed the two great kings of Prussia are the best illustration

of this. They both felt that service to this impertinently demanding but (through reason) compelling idea of the Prussian state to be
something they had not sought, something imposed upon them,
and indeed something alien to their personalities; and both of
them were remoulded and disfigured in their character by that
service – often in an evil sense. Frederick Wilhelm I, for instance,
had the strange habit of referring to the King of Prussia in the
third person: 'I want to be the Field Marshal and Finance
Minister of the King of Prussia; that will be of great advantage
to the King of Prussia.' And this tyranny of the King of Prussia,
to which he submitted, presently turned the simple, pious, up-
right, blustering but basically kind-hearted man into a tyrant
himself. It introduced the elements of driving and being driven
into everything he did and into his style of government: his never
being satisfied, his violence, his short temper, his wild threats,
his régime of flogging, his impatience, the perpetual 'Cito!
Citissimo!' under his edicts. When certain War Councillors or
Domain Councillors raised some objections to a royal decree this
King of Prussia exploded: 'These people want to force my hand:
they shall dance to my tune or I'll be damned: I shall order
hangings and roastings like the Tsar and will treat them as rebels!'
And then suddenly the private Frederick Wilhelm breaks through:
'God knows that I am doing it unwillingly and that, because of
those sluggards, I have not slept properly for two nights.' A good-
natured man turned into a tyrant by service to the state.

That was Frederick Wilhelm I. How much more did it apply
to Frederick the Great! His dictum, 'The King is the first servant
of the state', repeated frequently and in different contexts, is
well known; what is less well known is that in the French original
the word is not '*serviteur*', as on some subsequent occasions, but
'*domestique*' – '*le premier domestique de l'État*', the first footman
of the state. It suddenly has quite a different ring and echoes
another dictum of Frederick's which he likewise repeated in
many variations: 'How I abominate this trade to which the blind
chance of my birth has condemned me!'

Frederick was an artistic person by nature, a 'philosopher'
(today one would say an intellectual) and a humanist. That was

what, during the time he was Crown Prince, brought him into terrible conflict with his father, a conflict which we do not propose to relate here for the hundredth time. His uniform, in later life his invariable attire, he at first, in disgust, called a 'dying outfit'. His flute playing, his love of the arts, his *Anti-Machiavelli*, positively dripping with enlightened humanism, his enthusiastic friendship with Voltaire, the flood of humanitarian decrees when he assumed the throne – abolition of torture (with certain exceptions), 'Journals must not be interfered with', 'In my state let everyone find salvation in his own fashion' – this was not a mask or a magnanimous whim, but the real Frederick, his original character. He sacrificed it to the 'abominable trade' to which he found himself condemned – or, more accurately, to the Prussian *raison d'état* which demanded that he pursue power politics, wage wars, fight battles, conquer territories, break alliances and treaties, counterfeit money, extract the last ounce of effort from his subjects and his soldiers, and ultimately also from himself – in short, to be the King of Prussia. He became bitter. He did not rave like his father but he became an icy cynic, a malicious tormentor of those around him, loving no one, loved by no one, bitterly indifferent to his own person, ill-kempt, unclean, always wearing the same shabby uniform; yet still full of spirit even though this was a hopeless spirit of negation; profoundly unhappy, yet at the same time indefatigably active, always on duty, always at his post, untiringly practising his abominated trade, a great king to his last breath, a king with a broken soul.

We cannot deny ourselves a quotation from Frederick's writings – twenty-five volumes, nowadays virtually all unread, unjustly so. This is a quotation from a private letter which, so it seems to us, offers a glimpse of the most secret aspect of this royal character. 'If I do not speak about Providence,' Frederick the Great writes, 'then this is because my rights, my quarrels, my person and the entire state seem to me to be matters too slight to be of importance to Providence; the worthless and childish squabble of humans does not merit its concern, and I do not think that it would perform any miracles to see Silesia in the hands of the Prussians rather than those of the Austrians, the Arabs or the Sarmatians; I there-

fore do not abuse such a sacred name for such an unholy object.'
That is what he really thought, and yet he sacrificed countless
human lives to that unholy object – including, in a sense, his own.

One might find this cynical or entrancing. Frederick is what
the English call an 'acquired taste': repulsive on first contact, yet
as one gets involved with him one becomes addicted to him and
finds him arousing a sentiment that cannot be called love but that
may possibly be stronger than love. Those patriotic and devout
adulatory stories that used to be recounted in vast numbers and
that turned 'old Fritz' into a popular anecdotal hero seem merely
ludicrous when one has taken a closer look at the real Frederick;
but the present fashion of writing about him in a derogatory
manner in a strange way fails to reach its target. He is immune
from such defamatory zeal, as though he had known all this himself, and a lot better at that. In the end, when the worst has been
said, he remains as fascinating as ever. Much the same is true of
his state – his and his father's state. Something of the character of
the two kings – father and son – went into it. A rugged rational
state, crudely carpentered, without the charm of Austria, the
elegance of Saxony, the unspoilt natural vitality of Bavaria – one
might say: a state without qualities – and yet 'quite something'.
Viewed from outside classical Prussia aroused no enthusiasm – if
anything it aroused dislike, or at best respect. But the closer one
looks at it the more interesting it becomes.

The most accurate characterization of this state is in a book
which, unfortunately, has attracted little notice, *Germans and
Slavs* (1974), by Arno Lubos, a Silesian scholar of German and
Slav affairs. The following quotation is long but it is worth reading and rereading, and slowly: every words hits the target. Lubos
views the Prussian state from the point of view of the many Poles
who, in the last third of the eighteenth century, became involun-
tary Prussians. This is as he sees it:

Prussia at that time presented itself as an extraordinary state of discipline, submission to authority, military drill, impeccable officialdom,
a loyal aristocracy, an incorruptible enlightened humanitarian juris-
diction, undiscriminating reason, a perfect administrative apparatus, a

self-denial-demanding Calvinist and Protestant-stamped Puritanism, and a cosmopolitan and intra-denominationally liberal trend. A vast conglomeration of ideas, created by four very unlike rulers, offered itself as an entity under the concept of crown and territory. Prussia was characterized by the fact that – in contrast to ethnically-based countries – it had to produce state-shaping and state-promoting maxims and that it existed only through these, that it possessed a never disputed variety and, as a counterpoise, developed a particularly drastic authoritarian principle. There was no Prussian ethnic element, no exemplary preferential position of a heartland ethnic unit, no uniform dialect, no dominant folklore. Indeed this variety might be seen as its essential characteristic, even though it meant that the uniting and levelling authority of the crown and the state organization had to be emphasized. Yet that authority was derived not from historical or dynastic titles but reciprocally from the viability of the state as an entity, from the performance of the ruling house, of the subordinate institutions and the strata of the people. The state defined itself by the duty, which it assigned to everyone, to take his place in it and be active for it. It promised power-political, economic, social and cultural progress on the basis of a universal will to be efficient. It punished the negation of that will to be efficient as a threat to its existence. It demanded total avowal, absolute submission and readiness for service. It conceded freedoms in so far as these were grounded in the state, e.g. in its denominational and ethnic multiplicity. Prussia imposed a new communal attitude especially upon the Slav minority.

It would be impossible to sum up the nature of classical Prussia more accurately – it is really all that needs saying. Nevertheless we shall take a somewhat closer look at the reasons for all this and see how the individual features came about.

The most conspicuous feature of classical Prussia in the view of its contemporaries and of posterity, though listed by Lubos as only one among others, was of course its militarism. Prussia, more than any other, was a military state. It had to be one if its unconnected constituent parts were to be turned into a cohesive territorial body – and this was the rational requirement of its position.

'Other states possess an army; Prussia is an army which possesses a state', Mirabeau wrote, half scoffing and half horrified, during the late years of Frederick the Great. That is both correct and incorrect. The Prussian army never 'possessed' the Prussian state, it never made the slightest attempt to govern it or to determine its policies, it was the best disciplined army in the world; a military *coup d'état* was always inconceivable in Prussia. On the other hand, the army was the state's most important instrument, its trump card and its darling; everything was done for it, everything revolved about it, everything stood or fell by it. Prussia was indeed 'possessed' not by the army but by its care for the army. Even its – in its day highly modern and progressive – financial, economic and population policies ultimately served the end of military prowess and that meant its army.

Admittedly Prussia was merely doing to an exaggerated degree what had become the universal usage in Europe at the time. Prussian militarism was no isolated phenomenon; in this respect, too, Prussia was supported by the eighteenth century's spirit of the age. It merely drew the most radical conclusions from the military revolution which had taken place in all great European states following the Treaty of Westphalia.

That revolution, briefly, aimed at the nationalization of the armed forces. Until then, strange as this may seem to us today, the European states had not possessed armies – at most royal lifeguards and militias. Armies were private enterprises, and whenever a state needed an army to wage a war it would hire one – frequently without being able to pay for it. This system, whereby the numerous wars of the sixteenth and seventeenth centuries had been waged, including the Thirty Years' War, was not successful in the long run – in the Thirty Years' War, in fact, it led to disastrous results for the warring countries. Discipline in the mercenary armies, with their often irregular pay, was poor, and they also lacked what is nowadays called logistics – an organized and secure source of supplies for their needs. (Wallenstein's army, at least in its initial period, was a forward-looking exception in this respect.) They had, on their own initiative, to live off the land in which they were fighting or camping, or through which they were marching; they devastated these countries and in the Thirty Years' War utterly destroyed entire regions.

After that war the system was universally discarded and the

opposite extreme was frequently adopted. The armies which all states that considered themselves respectable now created were equipped with their own state-controlled system of supplies; they no longer lived off the land but marched from depot to depot (which greatly impaired their manoeuvrability in the wars of the eighteenth century), and were subjected to the most ruthless and barbaric discipline that soldiers ever had to endure. Nowadays we are horrified when we read of the flogging and gauntlet-running in eighteenth-century armies (not only the Prussian). But one must also see the other side: the soldiers now had to suffer more, but the civilian populations suffered less. In the age of the undisciplined, unsupplied mercenary armies warfare had meant perpetual burning, looting, murder and rape. That was now over. Frederick the Great, without departing too far from the truth, was able to declare: 'The peaceful citizen should not even notice that the nation is at war.' This was fewer than a hundred years after the Thirty Years' War.

That Prussia should participate in this all-European military revolution, and that it should, just as did Sweden, France, Spain, Austria and Russia, become a military state was not in itself remarkable. But three things were remarkable: first the size of the Prussian army, second its quality, and third its social composition.

The Prussian army had been increased to a peacetime strength of 83,000 men under King Frederick Wilhelm I, the 'soldier king'; his successor increased it to 100,000 the moment he came to the throne, and doubled that figure later when he waged war. That was a disproportionate number for a small country, an incredible number; much larger states such as France, Austria and Russia maintained only slightly bigger armies. It required spartan economy ('Prussian thrift') in all other state expenditure; four-fifths of the state's revenue was spent on the army. The Prussia of the 'soldier king' deliberately sacrificed splendour to power, to 'what really counts', as the king put it. His court, in an age which attached the greatest importance to courtly magnificence elsewhere, appeared downright beggarly; desperately little was done for the arts or the promotion of culture under his reign, and

35

the contrast between Prussian poverty and Prussian militarism was the subject of general derision and head-shaking in Europe.

But that was the least of it. Thrift alone was not enough to meet the costs of such an exceptional military power in such a poor state. Not for nothing had Frederick Wilhelm declared himself the 'Field Marshal *and Finance Minister*' of the King of Prussia. Under his reign Prussia became the most heavily taxed country in Europe, and Frederick the Great subsequently tightened the fiscal screw even further, thereby – in spite of his glory, to which his subjects were not unresponsive – making himself exceedingly unpopular in the long run. And these heavy taxes (consumer tax or '*Akzise*' in the towns, land tax or '*Kontribution*' in the countryside) had to be collected and enforced. This required an efficient financial administration – a large civil service which could only be paid with Prussian thrift yet had to be absolutely reliable. This in turn made it necessary to subject it to a well-nigh military discipline (and a quasi-military code of honour), and thus one thing led to another: the Prussian military state to the Prussian civil service state.

And similarly to the Prussian economy state. If the expensive army was to be paid and if, moreover, a war chest was to be accumulated, the population had to be heavily taxed. But if these taxes were to produce revenue then there had to be something to be taxed: a hungry cow does not yield much milk. So the Prussian state pursued a specific economic policy, financing and subsidizing manufactures on a scale unusual for the time – rural manufactures such as linen and wool weaving (needed also for clothing the army), urban manufactures such as the famous Royal Porcelain Manufactory in Berlin. It set up a state bank, concerned itself with land improvement and development (the drainage of the Oder marshes) – altogether a highly modern and progressive policy for its day, and, what is more, a humane one. It created work and livelihood. But only as a byproduct.

The same cool 'byproduct' humanity marked Prussian immigration and population policy; this will now have to be discussed in somewhat greater detail. For here we come to one of the fundamental features of classical Prussia, a feature just as typical and striking as its militarism: its well-nigh unlimited xenophilia, its unbounded readiness to accept immigrants and refugees. Many who find Prussian militarism repulsive regard this as a reconciling feature. But in fact the two belong together.

Prussia in the eighteenth century was a sanctuary and an asylum for the persecuted, the outcasts and the humiliated from all over Europe, almost as America was in the nineteenth century. That began under the Great Elector. When France in 1685 rescinded the Edict of Nantes, which had granted religious freedom to the French Protestants for a century, the Great Elector replied with the Edict of Potsdam which invited the persecuted to Prussia; and they followed that invitation in their thousands and were grateful for it. About the year 1700 one inhabitant of Berlin in every three was a Frenchman. The refugees were well treated, they received accommodation and credits, and they were in no way compelled to deny their nationality; they were even given their own French cathedral and their French grammar school. All quite exemplary. And profitable. It is common knowledge that the 'French colony', which survived in Prussia down to our own century, brought with it many refinements in trade and lifestyle and for several generations provided the state with outstanding servants and poets.

The French were not the only ones. In 1732, under Frederick Wilhelm I, there was another mass immigration wave: 20,000 Salzburg Protestants fled to Prussia to escape the Counter-Reformation and were settled in East Prussia which had been depopulated by the plague. Alongside these spectacular mass movements a steady stream of refugees and religious persecutees arrived in Prussia throughout the eighteenth century – and indeed earlier, ever since the days of the Great Elector: Waldensians, Mennonites, Scottish Presbyterians, also Jews, even occasional Catholics who were not happy in more strictly Protestant states. They were all made welcome and they were all allowed to continue to speak their own language, to practise their own customs and to 'find salvation in their own fashion'. Every new subject was welcome to the Prussian state. Nor was it ungenerous about accepting outstanding foreigners, if they so wished, straight into the upper echelons of its service. We shall discover later that the great men of the Prussian reform era – Stein, Hardenberg, Scharnhorst, Gneisenau – were nearly all of them non-Prussian in origin. And another thing we should state here, in anticipation: the millions of Polish subjects which Prussia acquired through conquest towards the end of the eighteenth century were never in the least harassed or discriminated against on grounds of nationality or religion. In the old Prussia – unlike the subsequent new German Reich – there was no question of 'Germanization'. Prussia was not a nation state and did not wish to be one; it was quite simply a state and no more – a rational state, open to anyone. Equal rights for everybody. And, of course, equal duties.

It all seems very pleasant and humane. And so it was. But humaneness was not Prussia's motive behind this exceedingly liberal immigration and population policy. Humaneness was a byproduct. The motive was statecraft; and if one looks a little more closely one again encounters that 'militarism', that excessively big Prussian army from which everything else followed.

The army was expensive – it consumed the state budget. In consequence higher tax revenue was needed; but higher tax revenue meant a growing fiscal and economic strength. Hence a specific economic policy was pursued and economic growth promoted, but this demanded a population increase. The time had not yet come when human labour could be replaced by machinery; hence an immigration policy was implemented – and if this also happened to be a humane policy, so much the better. 'Men I esteem above the greatest riches,' declared Frederick Wilhelm I, and Frederick the Great was even more explicit: 'The first principle, the most general and most true, is this: that a state's true strength lies in its large population.' In his Testament of 1752 (Bismarck later thought that this document should be kept secret for ever) he also uttered his ulterior motives: 'I wish we had provinces enough to maintain 180,000 men, that is 44,000 more than at present. I wish that after deduction of all expenditure an annual surplus of five million might be achieved. . . . That five million roughly amounts to the cost of a campaign. With that sum one might foot the costs of the war from one's own revenue without getting into financial embarrassment or becoming a burden to anyone. In times of peace that revenue could be used for all kinds of useful expenditure for the state.'

Thus in Prussia everything sooner or later leads back to the army, and we too must now return to it.

Measured by the population total and financial strength of the state, the Prussian army was undoubtedly monstrously over-proportioned – but it was, of course, numerically still smaller than the armies of the real great powers, France, Austria and Russia. That it should later prove equal to these bigger armies – in the Silesian Wars to just one of them and in the Seven Years' War to the three of them together – indicates a superior quality. The secret of that qualitative superiority has never been fully solved, neither then nor now. It can only partially be explained by the extraordinarily open-minded attitude of the Prussian generals towards the modest military-technological progress then possible. True, the Prussians were the first to introduce marching in step and to replace the wooden ramrod by an iron one. The famous or notorious Potsdam 'guard of giants' can also be considered from this point of view – a longer reach was obviously an advantage in bayonet fighting, and to that extent the 'soldier king's' collector's zeal for 'long fellows' was possibly more than just a fad. But that does not explain everything. The Prussian army's tactics and drill were the same as in all other armies, and its discipline, though strict enough, was no stricter than elsewhere. The familiar phrase 'The Prussians don't shoot fast' does not refer to their firing in battle – as a matter of fact they fired particularly fast in battle, with their iron ramrods – but to the fact that they were not in such a hurry to shoot deserters as, for instance, the French were, who mercilessly put their recaptured deserters up against the wall. In Prussia such unfortunates were beaten half-dead but then nursed back to health again so they could serve once more. They were far too valuable for execution – another aspect of Prussian thrift.

The real explanation of the superior quality of Frederick's army is probably different: it should be sought in its composition which had been progressively changing since the 1720s. Until then recruitment, as elsewhere, had been based exclusively on hiring men for money: soldiers were mercenaries, often foreigners, often social misfits. This accounted for the frequency of desertion and the inhumanity of discipline. The system never quite came to an end in the eighteenth century. Recruitment – a better term might be press-ganging – continued, costing a lot of money and causing a good deal of annoyance abroad, but during the second half of Frederick Wilhelm I's reign it was at first supplemented by levies and then, increasingly and gradually, replaced by them.

This began quite imperceptibly. At first only certain regions, 'cantons', were assigned to individual regiments for domestic recruitment, to ensure they did not poach from each other. Next a certain recruitment target was imposed on each canton, and from this, as early as the reign of Frederick Wilhelm I, developed a system approximating selective conscription.

Selective, by no means general as yet. Urban inhabitants were not levied at all, and even in the countryside there were numerous exceptions: tradesmen and craftsmen, the learned professions, landowning peasants, new settlers, workers in manufactures were exempted from military service once and for all; they had other tasks to perform for the state, such as to earn money and pay taxes. But the very fact of these numerous exemptions made it difficult for the non-exempted to escape 'recruitment', and thus recruitment in the countryside increasingly became a general levy, and the Prussian army increasingly became an army of the children of the country. And that, of course, made a difference to fighting morale.

In addition, however, it transformed the rural social structure of Prussia in a characteristic manner. (Again one thing was leading to another.) There gradually emerged a situation when it became a matter of course for peasants' younger sons who were not going to inherit a farm to join the army; and for the younger sons of Junkers who would not inherit estates to become officers. Needless to say, this consolidated Junkers power: the Junkers, in addition to being the feudal masters of their peasants, now also became their military superiors. At the same time it blunted the opposition between royal power and Junker power: as officers the Junkers became servants of the state – and developed a taste for it. The state, in turn, found it convenient to possess a reliable reservoir of officers among the Junkers.

Frederick Wilhelm I had still, in the traditional manner, been in a permanent state of conflict with his 'estates' (this in Prussia meant principally the Junkers). There is his well-known remark in connection with an East Prussian tax dispute: 'I am destroying the authority of the Junkers: I thus achieve my purpose and stabilize sovereignty as a brazen rock.' Not so Frederick the Great, who eventually exempted the Junkers from taxes altogether: 'For it is their sons who defend the country and their race is so good that it merits in every way to be conserved.' The aristocratic Prussian officers' corps thus became the bridge on which kingship and Junkerdom met: both now in the service of the state, in the service of a military state.

This peace between king and 'estates' is remarkable. It places Prussia in an exceptional position in the eighteenth century; elsewhere the conflict was still being exacerbated. Of course that peace had its price. It has been rightly said of classical Prussia that the state rested on two unequal legs – in the towns its power extended down to the last citizen; in the countryside it only extended as far as the Rural Councillor who, though a civil servant, invariably came from the local aristocracy and in a sense represented the link between state power and Junker power. Below the Rural Councillor the King had little influence in the countryside. On their estates the Junkers themselves reigned like little kings.

It has also been said that the Prussian peace between kingship and Junkers had been concluded on the backs of the peasants. On closer examination, however, it did not really change much for the peasants in their relations with the Junker class. In practice their sons now had to serve in the army just as did the sons of the Junkers. That was a new burden for both but also gave both, at least after some time, a new sense of value and honour. Otherwise everything remained as before. Relations between Junkers and peasants had not changed since the days of colonization. Both had come into the country, often together, as knights with their retinues; they had seized the land or had it assigned to them – the knights their estates and the peasants their farmsteads. True, the peasant families had to do double work: for themselves on their own farms, and also, obligatorily, on the Junkers' estates. So it had been from the beginning and so it continued into the nineteenth century. Peasant life was tough, in Prussia as elsewhere. Yet it is a noteworthy fact that the great German peasant wars of the sixteenth century stopped outside the colonial lands, and that even in the seventeenth and eighteenth centuries there was no perceptible class struggle in the countryside of Brandenburg or Prussia, no mass emigration and no drift from the land – that only erupted following Stein's unsuccessful emancipation of the peasantry, when peasants who under the old system often possessed land became free but landless agricultural labourers. The Prussian aristocracy, unlike its French, Austrian or even Polish counterpart, was not an urban or court aristocracy but a working landed gentry and was indeed often looked down upon as 'cabbage Junkers' or 'superior big peasants' by persons of quality in the Empire. There were no magnates in Prussia owning enormous estates. Symbiosis between the Junkers and 'their' peasants was close; to the peasant the Junker was not a remote anonymous exploiter but a manager known to him personally – as a rule respected and sometimes even popular. There were also 'slave-drivers'; but the mere fact that the term was used in Junker circles proves two things: that they were the exception rather than the rule and that they were disapproved of by their peers.

On the whole one does not get the impression that social conditions in the eighteenth-century Prussian countryside were intolerable for the peasants; they certainly were viable. And the fact that during the eighteenth century these relations were transferred to the military plane seems, if anything, to have raised the self-respect of the peasant soldier in an army soon to cover itself with glory. There is documentary evidence that while marching into the Battle of Leuthen the Prussian grenadiers were singing (it is always a good sign when an army sings), and that they were singing the verse of a hymn:

42

Grant that I do my duty as I see it,
As Thou for me, in my estate, decree it,
Grant that I do what must be done, with speed,
And when I do it that it may succeed.

This verse, incidentally, might have made quite a suitable Prussian anthem. The eighteenth-century Prussian state demanded from its subjects no fervour, it did not appeal to love of country or national sentiment, not even to tradition (after all, it had none), but solely to their sense of duty. The highest Prussian decoration, the Order of the Black Eagle, instituted by King Frederick I on the day before his self-coronation, bore the words '*Suum cuique*' – 'to each his own'. An appropriate slogan for his state. Perhaps even more appropriate if one translates it as 'To each his own duty'. The state assigned a task to each citizen, from the king down to the least subject, a task whose discharge was his strict duty, and each class had its own task. One had to serve with money, another with blood, a few with 'brain power', but all of them with application. In enforcing the implementation of these duties the state was merciless. Yet in every other respect it was again more liberal than any other state of its day – the liberality may have been cold and essentially based on indifference, but this did not make it any less beneficial to the citizen. We have already touched on Prussian immigration and asylum policy. 'To each his own' also meant: '*Chacun à son goût*'; anything that does not harm the state it will not interfere with. An extreme illustration is the true story of the cavalryman who had committed sodomy with his horse. Sodomy in eighteenth-century Europe was regarded as more or less the most hideous crime there was – punished everywhere by death in the most painful manner. Frederick the Great's judgement was: 'Have the swine transferred to the infantry.'

There were three great Prussian indifferences: the first seems exemplary to present-day liberals, the second questionable, and the third, if anything, distasteful. The eighteenth-century Prussian state was denominationally indifferent, nationally indifferent and socially indifferent. Its subjects could be Catholics or Protestants,

Lutherans or Calvinists, Jews or, if they wished, Muslims – all this was all right by the state, provided they punctually fulfilled their obligations to it. Equally it was nationally indifferent: they need not be Germans; French, Polish, Dutch, Scottish, Austrian immigrants were equally welcome, and when Prussia began to incorporate Austrian and Polish territories Austrians and Poles were also welcome subjects and were treated in exactly the same way as native Prussians. And it was socially indifferent: every Prussian subject was the master of his fate. How he coped with his life was his own business. Public welfare, such as it was, was confined to the war disabled and army orphans, and then not invariably. Frederick the Great expressly demanded equal rights even for the humblest beggar, but no more than equal rights – not welfare. If that beggar became a robber his right to equality became his right to face criminal proceedings. Anyone failing in civilian life could still be pushed into the army. If he did not do well even there, so much the worse for him.

The strange thing is only that these 'three indifferences' were judged to be exactly in the reverse order by contemporary observers.

The fact that Prussia was not what is nowadays called a welfare state was not resented by anyone: it was a matter of course. In eighteenth-century Europe the welfare state did not even exist as an idea. It was invented in the late nineteenth century, incidentally by a later Prussian statesman, Bismarck. The national state, likewise, had not yet been proclaimed anywhere, even though it existed latently in France, Britain, Spain, Holland and Sweden. Prussia's exceedingly generous immigration and nationality policy was not totally incompatible with European customs, and was, at most, seen as an exaggerated form of a practice not entirely unknown elsewhere. But the religious toleration practised in Prussia – that was unheard of in the eighteenth century and almost scandalous. In this respect Prussia was far ahead of its day – in a positive way, as most people would say today, in a negative way according to general opinion then. And that general opinion was not entirely unjustified, as it sensed correctly that Prussian religious toleration, certainly by the time of Frederick the

Great, essentially amounted to religious indifference – one might almost say contempt for religion – and that, to refer once more to Arno Lubos's résumé of the Prussian spirit, a puritanism of originally protestant cast was developing into a 'secular trend' for which God was dead and the state was tacitly assuming His place. Whether it was religious toleration or irreligion, the Prussian attitude to religion was, for its age, something at least as unusual and striking as Prussian militarism, and, since it represented a decisive feature of classical Prussia, we must examine it a little more closely.

There was something accidental about its origin, as about that of so much else in Prussia's genesis. We have mentioned old Johann Sigismund (1608–19), the gluttonous Elector of whom Frederick the Great said that the history of his house only began to be interesting after his accession because of his great eastern and western inheritances. Toleration started with him, and it was connected with the inheritances in the west. The territories of Jülich-Cleves on the lower Rhine, to which Johann Sigismund succeeded and about which there was a great deal of quarrelling (there were other rival claimants), were predominantly Calvinist, and Johann Sigismund was naturally anxious to win over Calvinist backing for his contested claim. So he had himself converted from Lutheranism to Calvinism. There may have been religious reasons involved, but the decisive ones, without any doubt, were political ones – bearing in mind that in the seventeenth century religion and politics were indissolubly intertwined. However, Johann Sigismund did not dare impose Calvinism on his Brandenburgian or East Prussian subjects. That might have led to incalculable difficulties, and he was a man who disliked difficulties. So he became the first German prince to waive his denominational authority – the principle of *cuius regio eius religio* – and Brandenburg-Prussia became the first country in which the coexistence of different religions was possible and indeed inevitable.

But it still caused difficulties: religious or denominational toleration was not something that came naturally to seventeenth-century people; it had to be imposed from above. They were accustomed to have their religion prescribed to them by the state.

45

But to have the state instead demand toleration of them, toleration of a different faith among their neighbours, a faith which to them was heresy – that offended their highest and most sacred sentiments. Calvinist preachers under the reign of Johann Sigismund had stones flung through their windows in Berlin. The clergy of all denominations had to be repeatedly forbidden by the Brandenburg Electors and Kings of Prussia, on pain of severe penalty, to fulminate or agitate from the pulpit against the devil's servants of a different faith.

The famous Berlin pastor and author of religious songs Paul Gerhardt preferred exile to submitting to such a violation of his conscience: he was a martyr to toleration. That religious toleration which to us now appears as Prussia's title to glory was to its subjects in the seventeenth century, and indeed well into the eighteenth century, a hard imposition, harder and less comprehensible than militarism, tax burdens and Junker rule.

Things only began to change in the second half of the eighteenth century when the Christian religion was losing its power and enlightenment seeped down to the population from above. Prussia with its denominational toleration was exceedingly well prepared for that change in the spirit of the age: it became the classical state of enlightenment, and no one could personify the new spirit more credibly or impressively than Frederick the Great, himself a freethinker whose derisive remarks about traditional religion and its institutions occasionally went beyond the boundary of good taste (such as his remark to the pious General Ziethen, who arrived late at Court and apologized that he had been taking Holy Communion: 'I trust, Ziethen, that you have well digested the body of your Saviour?'). Now at last toleration, instead of being something enforced and reluctantly accepted, became something desired and gratefully welcomed in many circles. But it should not be overlooked that it developed, if not into downright irreligion, then at least into religious indifference, and that the sense of duty to the state became stronger than that of duty towards God.

We are here on shaky ground: psychological processes and changes in attitudes can only be surmised and not attested.

Certainly there continued to exist in the Prussian provinces a widespread popular piety (later in the nineteenth century, even a religious resurgence), but was that really still Christian piety? It should not be forgotten that Christianity came late, very late, to the lands of Prussia, and often in a rather horrible way. No sooner had they become Catholics than the Prussians were made Protestants; and no sooner had they become Protestants than a religious toleration was forced upon them which in turn questioned the absolute validity of the Protestant faith. Is it surprising, therefore, that whereas religion held a firm place among older nations, in Prussia there was a certain vacuum which was filled by something that one might term state ethics? True, the Prussian Grenadiers marching into battle at Leuthen still sang a hymn – but its sole content, significantly, was a prayer for strength to do their duty, and the duty before them was the winning of a battle. Doing one's duty became the first and supreme commandment in Prussia and simultaneously its own doctrine of justification: whoever was doing his duty was not committing a sin, no matter what he was doing. A second commandment enjoined that one must never be sorry for oneself, and a third commandment, somewhat less pressing, directed that one should be perhaps not exactly kind – that would be going too far – but decent to one's fellow beings. Duty to the state came first. This substitute religion was something one could live with, even quite honestly and decently – so long as the state which one served was itself honest and decent. The limits and risks of that Prussian religion of duty only became fully apparent under Hitler.

If we were aiming at completeness we should now have to say a few words about public education and the administration of justice in Prussia, both of them primitive if compared with present conditions but, in their own day, rather ahead of the norm. But we are not seeking completeness. The essential points about the rugged rational state, into which Prussia developed in the eighteenth century, have been made. All that remains is to sum up our impressions. How does that state strike us today?

First of all as strange. Prussia has so little in common with our present-day liberal, democratic, national, social or cultural

47

ideas of a state that one is bound to ask oneself in astonishment:
did it all really happen only two hundred years ago? But let us
not forget that the same applies to all other eighteenth-century
European states (and, of course, far more so to non-European
ones). Anyone measuring the past by the yardstick of the present
merely displays his lack of a sense of history. As it is, it is rather
unfair, though of course inevitable, that it is always the present
that writes the history of the past and never the past that writes
our present history. An eighteenth-century Prussian confronted
with twentieth-century German history would shake his head over
a good many things, and wring his hands over some of them.

The second reaction produced by a contemplation of the
Prussian rational state is undoubtedly respect for the achievement,
and indeed aesthetic pleasure over the work of art that it represents. The way one thing follows from another, the way one
thing slots into another, how it all comes together and serves the
same purpose, the neat and solid way this crudely constructed
state machine functions, and indeed almost by itself, thanks to
its well-thought-out mechanism, without arbitrary intervention
or needless cruelty, and often even with cool humanity as a
byproduct – all that is marvellous to contemplate and excites the
same aesthetic pleasure as a perfectly composed fugue or a completely resolved movement of a sonata, or indeed as one of those
ingenious mechanisms of the early industrial age. There is a great
deal of genius in that rugged state and it is not impossible to feel
enthusiastic about it.

But some doubts suddenly arise, doubts which call a halt to
the enthusiasm. They are not so much reservations as this
question: What was it all in aid of? Prussia enjoined its subjects
to do their duty, but what duty did it fulfil itself? They all had
to serve the 'Prussian idea'; but what idea did Prussia serve?
We cannot discover any – either religious, or national, or even of
the kind nowadays called ideological. This state served only
itself, it served its own preservation which, unfortunately, given
geographical circumstances, inevitably meant its aggrandisement.
Prussia was an end in itself; to its neighbours it was a danger
and a threat from the very beginning. One could imagine Europe

without it; and it is not surprising that many hoped for just that, as early as the reign of Frederick Wilhelm I, when he made himself so alarmingly powerful, and even more so under Frederick the Great, when he put that power to use – to rapacious use, as one is bound to observe objectively. In Frederick the Great's wars right was almost invariably on the side of his enemies. And yet the injustice of the hero of those wars, Frederick, is overlooked due to his deeds of heroism. History is sometimes very unjust.

Prussia need not have existed. The world could have done without it. But it wanted to exist. No one had invited that small country into the circle of the European great powers. It demanded acceptance and it pushed its way in. The way it managed to do this in the course of half a century, with spirit, cunning, impertinence, insidiousness and heroism was a remarkable spectacle.

3

THE SMALL GREAT POWER

Favour of Circumstances – Frederick the Great's Adventures – An Underrated King of Prussia – Prussia as a Two-Nation State

THE DEEDS OF FREDERICK THE GREAT are, in their rough outline, still well known. He snatched Silesia from the Austrians and West Prussia from the Poles – both without legal or moral pretext – and thereby, at long last, gave his state a coherent territorial body, at least in the region of the east Elbe. His really great feat was that he successfully defended his rape of Silesia – for that is what it was – against a coalition of three great European powers, Austria, France and Russia, in the Seven Years' War. That was an achievement which, properly speaking, vastly exceeded the strength of a still small and rather poor Prussia and, even though favoured at the end by an unforeseen piece of good luck, bordered on the miraculous. It was this last achievement – not its area or population which, even including Silesia and West Prussia, were still rather modest – that placed Prussia in the same league as the European great powers, albeit as the last and smallest of them. After all, a state which throughout seven years had waged a war, undefeated, against three great powers must be a great power itself, improbable as this may have seemed in the case of Prussia.

A later Prussian statesman, Wilhelm von Humboldt, wrote in 1811, (at a time when Prussia's greatness seemed to be more or less at its end): 'Prussia cannot be compared to any other state; it is greater, and not only desires to be but must be greater than its natural weight entails. Something, therefore, must be added to that natural weight. . . . In the days of Frederick II it was his genius.'

There is a good deal of truth in this, but it is not perhaps the whole truth – leaving aside the question of whether Frederick's particular kind of greatness is accurately labelled by the word 'genius'. There is no doubt that, by means of personal daring, resolution and toughness, Frederick had extracted from Prussia a performance which went beyond the mere material strength of the country and could not be repeated at will. Still, Frederick had greatly enlarged, indeed almost doubled, Prussia's material base of power; and after his death, under successors whom no one would credit with 'genius', Prussia maintained itself as a great power first for a period of twenty years and later, after an admittedly sudden and heavy fall, re-established itself as a great power. So there must have been some other contributory factors, apart from Frederick's personal qualities and achievements, to lend great-power quality to that inconspicuous political structure. And these other factors are clearly identifiable on closer inspection. There were two of them.

The first was the peculiar nature of the Prussian state which lent it a special elasticity and capacity for expansion, enabling Prussia better than any other state not only to conquer alien territories and populations but, following such conquest, to assimilate and integrate them successfully.

The second was the favour of circumstances: an unconsolidated, virtually fluid, international constellation of powers that offered more than the usual opportunity to a policy of bold action and rapid change of course, as practised by Frederick (and indeed, though rarely mentioned, by his first successor).

We shall return to the first of these factors at the end of this chapter, when we shall be considering the problems of the second and third partitions of Poland. The second factor should be borne in mind if one wishes to understand Frederick the Great's success and not merely shake one's head over it in amazement.

In its genesis and its rise to greatness Prussia was wholly a child of the European epoch between the Treaty of Westphalia and the French Revolution. At no other time could a state like Prussia have made such an unprecedented career. That period might be called the age of puberty of European power politics, an age of uncontrolled urges and wild pranks. In it the balance of power in Europe changed in a more kaleidoscopic manner than ever before or since.

Until then there had only been two real powers in Europe (also for a century and a half and, incidentally, curiously analogous to the present day) to whose overt or latent long-term conflicts all others had to be subordinated: Habsburg and Bourbon. Subsequently, from the end of the Napoleonic crisis to the First World War, Europe lived within a stable five-power system that was carefully kept in balance. But between 1648 and 1789 Europe was like a gambling room. Throughout 140 years the continent resembled a political stock exchange where quotations fluctuated all the time. Somewhere or other there was always a war. War at that period was virtually the normal state of affairs, even though (thanks to the military revolution mentioned in the preceding chapter) a fairly tolerable state during which peaceful citizens continued to live almost as in peacetime. The armies alone fought the war. That provinces and countries should change their rulers was nothing extraordinary in view of so many wars – any more than that new powers should arise and old ones decline.

The German (or Holy Roman) Empire had been a living corpse since the Treaty of Westphalia, a corpse within whose decaying body such structures as Bavaria, Saxony, Hanover and indeed also Brandenburg-Prussia were able to develop a vigorous life of their own. The Empire no longer counted as a power. But the two ancient principal powers, France and Austria, were joined by two new ones – England and Russia. Three old powers – Spain, Poland and Turkey – were losing strength and weight, and gradually deteriorated from being conquering and ruling states to being the pawns of foreign powers. Two new (though suspiciously puny) countries – the Netherlands and Sweden – temporarily rose to great-power status but were unable to maintain themselves at that height. As they began to decline a new and even ranker outsider appeared on the scene and, against all the odds, maintained its position – Prussia.

Against this background Frederick's territorial annexations do not look quite as blatant as when measured by present-day attitudes. After all, Frederick's Prussia was acting no differently in Silesia and West Prussia from the way France had acted or was acting in Alsace, or Sweden in Pomerania, or Bavaria in the Palatinate, or others elsewhere. Besides, at least in the case of West Prussia, it had the excuse that Prussia genuinely needed that link between Pomerania and East Prussia – a glance at the map would prove this.

Silesia, on the other hand, it did not need. By seizing Silesia, which projected like a long nose from the Brandenburg-Pomeranian-Prussian territorial mass in the north, Prussia was advancing into regions where, strictly speaking, it had no business. For centuries, as part of the Crown of Bohemia, it had belonged to Austria, and its seizure was a barefaced challenge to Austria, who never forgave the rape of Silesia – at least not for half a century, and deep down in its heart probably never. And let us not forget that Austria was, and for a long while remained, a far greater and stronger power than Prussia. By making a long-term enemy of Austria Frederick imposed upon his state a heavy mortgage which more than outweighed his territorial gain.

Why did he do it? As is well known, it was more or less his first action. He had come to the throne in the summer of 1740. By December he had ordered his army into Silesia, 'for a rendezvous with glory'. Why?

The vague inheritance claims which, at most, he could make on a few small parts of Silesia were too threadbare to be seriously regarded as a motivation, let alone a justification. He himself did not use them as an excuse. Reading his own explanations from the year 1740–41 one finds one's hair standing on end: 'The satisfaction of having my name in the journals and later in history seduced me' (in a letter of 1740). And a year later, in a draft for the *History of my Age*: 'Possessing troops ready to strike, a well-stocked state treasury and a lively temperament: these were the reasons that induced me to go to war.' But one must not take this quite seriously. Self-irony and self-mocking were part of Frederick's make-up. His real reasons for going to war, though opportunist enough, were nevertheless a little more serious. What 'seduced' him was a unique opportunity.

The Habsburg sovereign had died in October without male issue. The succession by his daughter, Maria Theresa, might be contested – or at least a price might be exacted for its recognition, such as, for instance, Silesia. And why not make doubly sure by first grabbing the price demanded and then, possession being the better part of the law, negotiating about it? The opportunity for that was also favourable since Silesia in 1740 was denuded of all Austrian troops and its capture was a military walkover. Austria had only just ended a not very happy war against the Turks with a not very happy peace, and 'after the conclusion of that peace the Austrian army was in a totally unsettled state. . . . The army was both diminished and discouraged. After the peace the major part of the troops remained in Hungary', to quote Frederick in his *History of my Age*. Austria was thus for the moment offering itself in a state of both susceptibility to political blackmail and military impotence – and Frederick just could not resist such an opportunity for achieving a massive territorial accretion to his country.

It was not ethical, nor can it be regarded as politically far-sighted. But that was the way politics was conducted in the eighteenth century, and not only by Prussia. It is significant that in the so-called War of the Austrian Succession, which was triggered off by Frederick's *coup*, it was not the Austrian victim but the Prussian aggressor that instantly found allies: France, Bavaria and Saxony. They all wanted to exploit Austria's momentary weakness. The fact that Prussia had exploited that weakness for a plain land grab did not in the least deter them from making common cause with it. Evidently they saw nothing wrong in that.

On the contrary, it was Frederick who eighteen months later coolly left his allies in the lurch. By then Austria was so hard pressed that it was forced to get some air somewhere. For the time being, the easiest move was to cede Silesia to the Prussians. Frederick for his part found his allies getting excessively powerful and a little alarming. As he himself wanted nothing more from Austria than Silesia he had no scruples about concluding a separate peace the moment there was no challenge to his possession of Silesia, even though on a provisional basis. Subsequently, when

Austria had once more gained the upper hand against the coalition weakened by his secession, Frederick, just as coolly as he had concluded it, tore up the recent peace treaty and resumed the war (1744) – after all, a victorious Austria might have taken Silesia back from him – but in 1745 broke his alliance with the coalition for a second time when Austria, for a second time, accepted his terms on Silesia. The War of the Austrian Succession eventually ended in 1748, after eight unprofitable years for all participants – except for Prussia which had left the war three years earlier, with its loot secure. A French diplomat of the time observed with witty disillusionment: '*Nous avons tous travaillé pour le Roi de Prusse*'. '*Pour le Roi de Prusse*' has since, in several European languages, become synonymous with 'for nothing.'

That was how politics was made in those days. Frederick's Silesian policy was undoubtedly unscrupulous power politics – but this was the style of the day. It became even clearer thirty-two years later when, at what is known as the first partition of Poland, he took Western Prussia as his share. The fact that in 1772 three great powers, in an era of absolute peace, agreed amongst themselves quite simply to carve out three suitable chunks from a weaker country lying between them seems monstrous to present ears. That it was not felt to be anything of the kind at the time emerges from the mere fact that three parties were sharing in the loot – not, as in the earlier case of Silesia, just one. The three, Russia, Prussia and Austria, evidently regarded their action as entirely in order, and no other power thought it sufficiently unusual or outrageous to feel obliged to intervene. Whether the idea was conceived by Russia or by Prussia is to this day a point of controversy. At all events the two quickly agreed, and Maria Theresa of Austria, who had had a few scruples initially, eventually participated in order not to be left empty-handed. Frederick's comment was: 'She cried but she took.'

A characteristic comment. Frederick the Great was a cynic. He was no more unscrupulous than other politicians of his day, but he differed from them in refusing to draw a cloak over his unscrupulousness. On the contrary, he positively took pleasure in openly calling the things he was doing (and which others, too, were doing) by their ugliest name – it is hard to say whether from exhibitionism or from a kind of inner despair over his 'abominable trade' (again his own words). There was undoubtedly a Mephisto-phelian streak in him. Whether one finds this repulsive or strangely attractive is a matter of taste. After all, there are quite a few readers of *Faust* who finds Mephistopheles more attractive than Faust and who inwardly applaud him whenever he reduces Faust's perpetual metaphysical tirades to their exceedingly earthly core by a cynical quip. But as a politician Frederick handicapped himself by his Mephistophelian cynicism, and this, in conjunction with his dare-devilry, nearly cost him his neck in the Seven Years' War. He was not a master politician. His greatness lay elsewhere.

A little while earlier we cautiously queried the term 'genius' which Wilhelm von Humboldt had used to characterize Frederick the Great. Frederick was witty, inventive, a man of many gifts, not only in political and military matters but also in the literary and musical fields. But he was not really a genius in any field – rather a highly gifted amateur in an exceptionally large number of directions. Just as his entirely respectable compositions do not begin to approach those of Bach, or his writings – though still very well worth reading – those of Voltaire, so as a politician and strategist he lacked the 'genius's' clarity of insight and overview, as well as the measured assurance in action which marks true greatness. On the contrary, certainly during the first half of his long reign, Frederick was time and again a downright gambler.

It was during this time that he earned himself the dual fame of the successful statesman and the victorious general. To the Germans of the later Prussian Empire he seemed, in a sense, Bismarck and Moltke rolled into one. But the comparison with Bismarck and Moltke, the moment it is seriously made, is un-favourable for Frederick. Bismarck's wars and Moltke's cam-paigns, whatever else one may think of them, were one and all masterpieces of planning and execution. Bismarck never started a war without first carefully isolating the prospective enemy and putting him in the wrong. Frederick in his three Silesian wars unconcernedly put himself in the wrong all the time; in the event of the Seven Years' War he launched an attack, with downright temerity, out of his own isolation on a greatly superior coalition whose very existence was largely his own work. Bismarck, in every war, knew from the outset how he might with advantage re-establish peace; Frederick never did. He 'put things to the test'.

What applies to Frederick the statesman also applies to Frederick the general. Moltke's campaigns were methodically calculated, carefully considered operations. Frederick's battles, with few exceptions, were strategic improvisations, not infrequently desperate gambles. This lent them a particular sparkle if things went well; if they went wrong the consequences were terrible. After Kunersdorf (1759) Prussia's situation was scarcely less desperate than forty-seven years later after Jena. Why the state should have collapsed after one of these defeats and not after the other is an interesting question to which we shall return. It was only partially due to Frederick's personal achievement.

But at least partially due. As for his title, 'the Great', he really only earned that during the long and terrible three final years of the Seven Years' War, not by genius but by strength of character. What Frederick displayed to the world and to posterity during those years was the spectacle of extreme perseverance, toughness and imperturbability in the total absence of hope; a spectacle of boundless steadfastness, in fact a kind of inner death from which every blow of fate recoiled. This king, who started as a frivolous 'pet dog of Fortune' (his expression), in misfortune behaved like a Red Indian at the torture stake. That was his real greatness. It is not diminished by the fact that it was rewarded by a saving stroke of good luck, Russia's change of reign and alliance.

The time has come to take a closer look at the history of the Seven Years' War. This war, the brilliant showpiece of 'Prussia's Glory', has been so wrapped up in later myth that its real course is scarcely perceptible. This myth was the beacon for twentieth-century Germans in two world wars, with disastrous consequences as we know. One more reason to clarify what really happened.

First its antecedents. The outbreak of the war was preceded by what contemporaries called a 'diplomatic revolution', a somersault-like reversal of traditional alliances. This was triggered off by Prussia. Its Silesian conquest had been made in alliance with France – an alliance which, as we have seen, Frederick kept or dropped as he pleased – and this Franco-Prussian partnership later became a permanent institution. In his political testament of 1752 Frederick had written:

> Especially since the acquisition of Silesia our present interest demands that we should remain in alliance with France and likewise with all enemies of the house of Austria. Silesia and Lorraine are two sisters, the elder of whom has married Prussia and the younger France. This compels us to the same policy. Prussia must not stand idly by if France were to lose Alsace or Lorraine, and the diversions which Prussia can stage in France's favour are effective in that they immediately carry the war into the heart of the Austrian hereditary lands.

Strange thoughts for those who wish to credit eighteenth-century Prussia with a 'German mission', but entirely convincing as political argument – so long as the ancient Franco-Austrian enmity continued.

But it did not continue. In place of the ancient continental hostility between France and Austria, which owed its continued existence to tradition rather than to any actual issue under dispute, a new hostility was increasingly emerging between France and Britain, with highly topical points of contention in America, Canada and India. And this new constellation was underestimated by Frederick when in January 1756 he concluded an alliance with Britain, the Treaty of Westminster. He miscalculated in two respects: he was hoping that Britain would draw Russia away from its alliance with Austria, an alliance which had been in existence for some time, or at least hold it in check – a vain hope; and secondly he calculated that France's conflict with Austria was insuperable (just as Holstein one-and-a-half centuries later was to take into consideration the conflict between Britain and Russia as a solid and invariable fact in his calculations). But here he miscalculated (as did Holstein), and France took umbrage. This gave Austria an opportunity to bury its old quarrel with France and for its part ally itself with its former enemy against Prussia. This was the second 'diplomatic revolution' of 1756.

Austria had never come to terms with the loss of Silesia. Even its alliance with Russia had served as a preparation for its reconquest in the future. The new triple alliance between Austria, France and Russia enabled the former to raise its sights: the reduction of Prussia to the Margravate of Brandenburg, and the share-out of the rest of its possessions among the allies. It cannot be said that these aims, given the crushing superiority of the grand coalition, were in any way unrealistic, nor that they transcended the framework of the power politics of the century. Why should Prussia not be partitioned the way Poland was to be partitioned later?

Frederick's position was grim. His new ally Britain was far away, the supposed British theatres of war were even further away, in India and Canada. He had to deal single-handed with three opponents, each of whom was stronger than he. His decision was for a preventive war.

But with characteristic temerity he also planned to turn the preventive war into a new war of conquest. Frederick's political testament of 1752, quoted earlier, contains these sentences: 'Of all countries of Europe those most to be considered by Prussia are Saxony, Polish Prussia and Swedish Pomerania. Saxony would be the most useful.' Frederick began the war by attacking Saxony without a declaration of war, occupying it and taking the Saxon army prisoner. Throughout the war he treated Saxony not as an occupied but as a conquered and annexed territory: the Saxons henceforward had to pay Prussian taxes, collected by Prussian officials, and the captured Saxon army was, without further ado, incorporated by the King of Prussia into his own army. This was not successful. The Saxon soldiers deserted whenever they could. They, too, had a sense of honour.

The war which began with Prussia's conquest of Saxony consisted of four periods of unequal length. First, for nine or ten months, Prussia was attacking; then, for two years, Prussia was defending itself with unexpected success; next came three long years of desperate hanging on and a well-nigh hopeless fight for Prussia's survival; and finally a year of mounting war-weariness, ending with a peace of exhaustion.

59

Prussia, wrote Carlyle, had a shorter sword than Austria, France and Russia, but unsheathed it more quickly. If Frederick's hopes were based on this, they deceived him. The conquest of Saxony in the autumn of 1756 had cost him precious time. True, he was still able to invade Bohemia the following spring, but there an equally strong battle-ready Austrian army was waiting for him, and the Battle of Prague – until then the greatest battle of the century, with approximately 60,000 men on each side – was no more for Prussia than what Schlieffen used to call an 'ordinary victory'. The Austrians withdrew in good order, took up defensive positions in Prague, and had to be besieged, while in the meantime a relief army was approaching. Frederick was compelled to split his army to ward off the relief of Prague, and for the first time had to risk an offensive battle with numerical inferiority: at Kolin, with 33,000 Prussians facing 54,000 Austrians. He lost, and that meant that he had to abandon the siege of Prague and withdraw from Bohemia. The idea of taking his enemy unawares by a preventive war had failed.

Strictly speaking, the war was lost at that point, because all had now unsheathed their swords and they were attacking from all sides: the French, together with a levy of German imperial troops – the Empire, too, had declared war on Prussia, because of the attack on Saxony – were approaching through Thuringia, the Austrians retrieved a poorly defended Silesia, and the Russians occupied a totally undefended East Prussia. But now the Prussians showed their mettle: moving this way and that, hither and thither, always with the same small but superb army, they took on each opponent singly and won, each time against a numerically superior enemy, three glorious victories: in the late autumn of 1757 at Rossbach in Saxony over the French, in the winter at Leuthen in Silesia over the Austrians, and in the summer of 1758 at Zorndorf in the New Mark (they had got that far) over the Russians. These three battles have been Prussia's greatest pride to this day, and they made Frederick famous and popular throughout the world, and even in Germany (Goethe said that they were enthusiastic for Frederick – 'what did we care about Prussia!'): here was a David who had slain three Goliaths.

But of course he had not slain them, and in the long run their superiority could not fail to have its effect. Besides, Austrians, Frenchmen and Russians also had their soldierly honour and did not content themselves with being eternal losers. Frederick's magnificent little army had been gradually bled white, and his replacements, which he had ruthlessly levied and recruited, no longer had the military quality of the cuirassiers of Rossbach and Zorndorf or of the grenadiers of Leuthen. At Kunersdorf on the Oder, where in 1759 the Prussians, once again with considerable numerical inferiority, risked a decisive battle – this time against the combined Austrians and Russians – they were crushingly defeated, and this was the end of successful all-round defence. From now onwards Prussia was able only to conduct a protracted war of attrition.

That it should have been able to do this throughout three hope-less years seems like a miracle. But it becomes less miraculous if one considers the character of eighteenth-century wars. Wars then were not people's wars. We recall Frederick's dictum: 'The peaceful citizen should not even notice that the nation is at war.' Well, he noticed it all right – by the increased taxes, the devalued currency, the heavier military levies. But the land was not devastated, the fields were being tilled and the harvest was brought in, business continued, and scholars did not allow the war to disturb their controversies. Some correspondence of that time has come down to us, for instance that between Lessing and Nicolai: the war is scarcely mentioned in it. Another strange feature is the matter-of-fact way in which conquered and defeated countries and provinces adjusted themselves to the changing power relationships of the day: the Saxons obediently paid their Prussian taxes (only the Saxon soldiers were prevented by their professional honour from serving the Prussians), the Silesians unhesitatingly again paid homage to their Empress the moment they were occupied by the Austrians, and afterwards just as readily paid homage to the King when the Prussians returned; the East Prussians paid homage to the Tsarina. The war, in a manner of speaking, passed over the heads of the people; they ducked and let the storm blow over. Only for the soldiers was the endless war hard, terribly hard; but they were subject to iron discipline and mutiny was unthinkable. And for the hard-pressed King of Prussia, who needed a new idea every day in order to continue existing, the hopeless war, with no end in sight, was hard too; but that King now showed what stuff he was made of.

Salvation came early in 1762 when the Empress of Russia died. Her successor, a somewhat confused gentleman and private admirer of Frederick, not only concluded an instant peace but even allied himself with his idol, and the Russian Army changed sides. That a thing like that should be possible is likewise part of the picture of eighteenth-century war. This Tsar, Peter III, was assassinated that same year and his far from mournful widow and successor Catherine, subsequently to be called 'the Great', terminated the Prussian alliance, that whim of her odd husband. But she did stick to the peace, and the other allies were increasingly leaning towards peace too. Their coffers were empty, their armies were exhausted, the outcome of the Franco-British war was decided, and that tough Prussia was evidently not to be finished off. Seven years is a long time, and an old war feels different from a young one. Anger and ambition evaporate among eternal troubles, worries and disappointments. As far as Frederick was concerned, he had long been fighting only for survival. Thus the Peace of Hubertusburg was concluded – a peace of exhaustion which left everything as it was. Saxony was restored, Silesia remained with Prussia; so of course did East Prussia. No one, it seemed, had won anything as a result of that war: they had all fought for nothing. But in effect the draw in which the war ended was a great triumph for Prussia: it had stood up to three great powers.

Did that make it a great power itself? That remained very doubtful for some time yet. Frederick himself, at any rate, always realized that, in spite of the military glory, he had ultimately got by through an unexpected piece of good luck. Even after the Second Silesian War he had said he would never again attack as much as a cat as long as he lived. After the Seven Years' War he meant it. He returned to his father's principles, which had consisted of making Prussia strong and ever stronger internally, without wasting that strength through putting it to excessive use.

One might say that during the second half of his long reign he became Prussia's second greatest domestic king. His foreign policy after 1763 – like that of his father – again became cautious, modest and defensive, anxious only to prevent Austria from once more becoming oppressive or over-powerful in the Empire, for instance by the acquisition of Bavaria. He was now looking for support, chiefly from Russia. 'It pays to cultivate the friendship of those barbarians,' he said in his best Mephistophelian style, thereby stating a political principle to which he adhered to the end, and to which Prussia adhered to its advantage for nearly a century. It did not do badly at all in the wake of Russia. But that was not really great power politics. Great power politics, though this is not generally known, were the prerogative of Frederick the Great's successor.

The Prussia which Frederick left was an oddity in Europe: a small great power or a semi-great power, looking on the map like a Turkish sabre or a boomerang: long and curved as a worm, virtually nothing but frontiers; plus some scattered possessions in western Germany, indefensible in the event of war. Prussia at the end of his reign was an uncertain quantity; on close examination still lacking any solid basis of power or even existence; just terribly prickly, with a tough drive for self-preservation and with that terrifying army, the grenadiers of Leuthen and Torgau who, a quarter century earlier, had been too much for the whole of Europe. So long as its grand old man was alive, and so long as, now grown cautious, he left others in peace, Prussia, in God's name, had better be left in peace too.

Nevertheless this was only a seeming peace. The new semi-great power in the north-east of Europe was living in an insecure halfway house that could not be a home in the long term; Prussia had to go forward or back. A small state with the army of a great power, the whole country nothing but frontier, the whole country nothing but garrison, and behind it always the knowledge that it might be wiped out, '*toujours en vedette*': in the long run this was untenable. There could only be a renunciation and back-tracking, or a move forward. Frederick's successor chose the latter.

That successor, Frederick Wilhelm II, 'Fat Wilhelm', has had a raw deal from Prussian historiographers. They never forgave him his mistresses and concubines, but he was not really a bad ruler at all; one might even argue that he was one of the most successful Hohenzollern kings. In character he was the exact opposite of his great predecessor: not a free-thinker and not an ascetic, but sensuous and religious (a common combination); a lover of art, kind-hearted, impulsive, enterprising, ambitious, and nobody's fool. The Prussia he left was not only much larger than the Prussia he inherited, it was also more relaxed, more self-assured and even more amiable. Under Frederick Wilhelm II there emerged, in this previously so sober and indeed impecunious and rugged state, a flowering of culture and a wealth of talent which continued for fifty years. And one cannot deny the King some credit for it: on his command Langhans built the Brandenburg Gate and Schadow put a quadriga on top of it; the Gillys, father and son – and later their successor Schinkel – gave Berlin the finest urban architecture it ever had; Iffland raised the Royal Theatre to the highest standard, just as Zelter did the Academy of Music, and if the King had had his way Mozart would actually have moved to Berlin, which might have prolonged his life. Under the reign of Frederick Wilhelm II Berlin also began to be the city of literary-political salons, and the headquarters of the German romantics. One might say that Frederick Wilhelm II, after nearly a century, again picked up the cultural tradition of the first King of Prussia. Admittedly, like that king, he was also a spendthrift. But then most princely patrons are.

In his foreign policy, however, he picked up the threads of the early years of Frederick the Great – which, let us not forget, had been years of high-spirited and indeed frivolous adventurousness. Just as did the young Frederick, Frederick Wilhelm II acted upon the principle (described as indispensable for a state in the position of Prussia by a French diplomat, Count Hauterive) 'that nothing could happen on the continent that did not concern him, and that no political event of any importance should take place without his participation'. In his early years he went too far in that respect. His intervention in the Netherlands, where he restored the House of Orange to the throne by force of arms (1787); and his intervention in an Austrian-Russian war with Turkey, which he stopped by the threat of war at the head of his mobilized army (Treaty of Reichenbach, 1790, sharply criticized by Bismarck), were acts of prestige policy rather than a policy of sober pursuit of his interests. Nevertheless the Treaty of Reichenbach was a prelude to a *rapprochement* with Austria from which, in 1792, sprang an ideological-monarchist alliance against revolutionary France. The war which followed from it (declared, incidentally, by France and not by the allies) went on, as is well known, with brief interruptions for a full twenty years. But not for Prussia.

Prussia, in 1795, suddenly performed a *volte-face*. She made a separate peace with France, on most favourable terms : the whole of northern Germany as far as the Rhine and the Main was neutralized under Prussian guarantee; it became what would nowadays be called a Prussian sphere of influence. At the same time, in the east, where there had been war between Poland and Russia since 1792 and where, in consequence, the final partition of Poland had become a topical issue – since there was little doubt about the outcome – Prussia now had a free hand, while Austria remained tied up in the war with France; with the result that this time the lion's share went to Prussia. Poland all the way to the Bug and to the Pilitza was annexed to Prussia. Prussia thus gained two huge new purely Polish provinces, South Prussia with its capital Posen and New East Prussia with its capital Warsaw. Almost the whole of the Polish heartland had thus become Prussian. And Prussia now was virtually a two-nation state.

At this point one should stop for a deep breath. Prussia as a two-nation state, a half-Polish Prussia – that surely in the light of its later history seems like a mirage, unreal, unnatural, a strange deviation from its path. And, of course, it only lasted for twelve years. Even so, it was not all that unnatural. After all, the real proto-Prussia, East Prussia and West Prussia, had long existed in closest union with Poland – East Prussia for nearly two hundred years as a secondary Polish territory, under royal Polish supremacy, and West Prussia actually for more than three hundred years as an integral part of Poland. Why then shouldn't this Polish-Prussian entity, now that power relations had changed, continue just as well under a Prussian label as it had done under a Polish one? Certainly a development of Prussia towards the east instead of towards the west was by no means as impossible as German nationalist historiography was to present it subsequently. To the age of nationalism, which began in the nineteenth century and which we have not yet quite outlived, a half-Polish Prussia was bound, and still is bound, to sound monstrous. But the eighteenth century saw nothing strange in two-nation or multi-nation states, and a political union of Prussia with, say, Bavaria, with which it had never had anything to do, would have then seemed far more improbable than a union of Prussia with Poland.

Be that as it may, two points have to be made: Frederick Wilhelm II had taken seriously 'Prussia's rise to great-power position' which his predecessor had inaugurated, and it was he who properly accomplished it; he had burst out of that Prussian halfway house in which Frederick, after the Seven Years' War, had remained for a quarter-century. The second point is that he was successful. Things may have been a little hectic; a lot of improvisation, a lot of rapid switching, a lot of to-ing and fro-ing. But in the end, undoubtedly, came a successful breakthrough. Anyone admiring the first eight years of Frederick the Great's reign – and all nineteenth- and twentieth-century Prussian his-toriography did so unanimously – cannot then reject Frederick Wilhelm's II's policy as a mistake or as the beginning of the decline – as in fact was done by almost everyone. It was the same policy. The same daring and reckless gamble for high stakes, the same blinding fireworks of diplomacy and military operations, the same swift change of positions and alliances, the same surprise *coups*; and the same success. Prussia in 1795 was no longer a semi-great power; in terms of territory and population it now possessed the foundations of genuine great-power status. It was no longer a thin crescent moon on the map but a solid chunk of territory (of about the size of the German Democratic Republic and today's Poland put together, with a few deductions); and to the west of this block the North German plain as far as the

Rhine and Main was, after 1795, no longer only dotted with Prussian enclaves but neutralized in its entirety under Prussian guarantee by a treaty with France: in other words a Prussian zone of influence. With only a little exaggeration one might say that Prussia dominated the entire territory from Warsaw to Cologne – the Polish territory directly, though by the grace of Russia; the German territory indirectly, though by the grace of France. The partnership established with Russia and France was not to be despised either: it provided a solid backing for Prussia's position of power. Prussia was no longer isolated in Europe; Austria was. It was unthinkable now that it could take Silesia back.

Why was this tremendous Prussian achievement of 1786–95 never acknowledged by German or Prussian historiography in the way the very similar achievements of 1740–48 and, later, of 1864–71 were? Because it was of shorter duration? But none of the Prussian successes was of very long duration. The main reason, surely, was different. Prussian-German historiography of the Treitschke school condemned it because in its eyes it was a mistake: the Prussian-Polish two-nation state was not compatible with Prussia's 'German mission'. And today one feels embarrassed about the partitions of Poland, one regards them as an injustice and indeed a crime against the Polish nation which, after all, had not been consulted.

But in those days nations never were consulted on whose rule they wished to live under – never and by no one – nor did they expect to be consulted. In the eighteenth century there was neither a German nor a Polish nationalism. Politics was the business of emperors and kings, and for populations to change their state and overlord in line with political developments was entirely customary; they accepted it and they were used to it. No one at the time was thinking about Prussia's 'German mission' – least of all the Germans and the Prussians themselves. As for the Poles, who in their own heyday had never hesitated about incorporating Lithuanian, Belorussian, Ukrainian and also German-settled territories (West Prussia), they were of course pained but hardly surprised to find, in a changed power situation, to have the same done to them by Russia, Prussia and Austria. Indeed they were glad to fall under the sway of Prussia or Austria rather than Russia – in much the same way as the Germans after 1945 were glad to come under a Western occupying power rather than the Eastern one.

It is true that by the end of the eighteenth century the idea of nationalism as something to catch the imagination of the masses was just round the corner. It was the French Revolution that brought it up, together with the equally new ideas of democracy and people's sovereignty. During the following period a lot of Germans became nationalists as a consequence of alien Napoleonic domination, just as a lot of Poles became nationalists as a direct result of the partition. A lot of them but by no means all. The conflict between the new nationalism and the old political order continued right through the nineteenth and – in Austria – well into the twentieth century; only recently has nationalism been widely victorious, at least as an idea. At the time of Frederick Wilhelm II, however, all this was still in the future, and it would have required exceptional far-sightedness to foresee it. The Prussia of the 1780s and 1790s cannot be blamed for acting in accordance with the ideas of its own day and not those of the nineteenth and twentieth centuries.

Admittedly it was more closely tied up with the ideas of that age – the age of its own emergence – than were other more ancient states, where echoes still lingered of the Middle Ages and of the age of religious wars. Prussia was modern – the most modern state of the period of the Enlightenment; one might also say with the cynicism of Frederick that Prussia in the eighteenth century was an article of fashion and fashionable articles quickly become obsolete when the fashion changes. We shall see in the next chapter the desperate efforts made by Prussia under Frederick Wilhelm II's successor to keep in step with the times, to be 'up to date', and we shall also see how the great system of reforms undertaken to that end was a failure in spite of all endeavours. But in 1790 and 1795 none of that had yet been thought of. Throughout Europe – except for France – this was still the age of the rococo, the last fine flowering of the Enlightenment, *raison d'état* and absolute monarchy; Prussia was totally and entirely the creature of that age, its purest incarnation: not a national state but a rational state. That perhaps was its weakness – but for a whole century it was also its strength.

It may be remembered that at the beginning of this chapter we briefly referred to the particular elasticity of Prussia, a rubber-like capacity to stretch which served it well throughout the century; and we then promised to return to this point later, in connection with the partitions of Poland. That moment has now come.

Prussia's success story in the eighteenth century – and it was undeniably a downright sensational success story – was due not only to the 'genius' of Frederick the Great, not only to favourable external circumstances and their skilful exploitation, and not only to the fortunes of arms and military prowess. It was above all due to the fact that the Prussia of that century was in such complete harmony with the spirit of the age. This rational state fitted perfectly into the age of reason. Nothing but a state and entirely a state: non-ethnic, non-tribal, abstract, a pure administrative, judicial and military system constructed from the spirit of the Enlightenment – all this made it possible for 'Prussia' to be moved about or transferred almost at will, to embrace, as it were, any nations, tribes or territories. A popular couplet of the day ran:

> No one becomes a Prussian without need for it,
> Having become a Prussian he thanks God for it.

This Prussian rational state – which Hegel later, maybe with some exaggeration but not without good cause, regarded as the most perfect realization of the idea of the state, the idea of the pure state, that had ever been produced by history – not only had a hardness, a metallic quality, something of a mechanical nature. It had all this, but it also possessed a cool liberality, justice and toleration which were no less welcome to its subjects for being, as we saw in the preceding chapter, based on a kind of indifference. In Prussia no witches were burned at a time when this was still common practice elsewhere, there were no forcible conversions and no religious persecution, anyone could think and write as he pleased, everyone was subject to the same law. The state was free from prejudice, it was rational, practical and just. So long as one gave unto the state the things that were the state's, it in turn gave 'to each his own'.

The millions of Poles, for instance, whom Prussia incorporated between 1772 and 1795, were no worse off in Prussia than before – if anything better. There was no intention to 'Germanize' them, such as became the sad practice in the German Reich in the days of Bismarck and even more so after Bismarck. If anyone in the eighteenth century had proposed to a Prussian that he should treat the Poles in the way Hitler treated them in the twentieth (and subsequently, as a counter-move, Poland treated the Germans under its administration) he would have been stared at by this eighteenth-century Prussian as if he were a lunatic. The Prussianized Poles were treated neither as sub-humans nor rejected as alien bodies; they were not interfered with or harassed in the least in the practice of their language, customs or religion; on the contrary, they were given more primary schools than they had had before, with teachers who of course had to speak Polish. Polish serfdom was replaced by the milder Prussian hereditary tenancy, and all Poles enjoyed the Universal Prussian Land Code, which came into force in 1794, a security before the law which they appreciated just as the Rhinelanders did the Code Napoléon ten years later. It is an interesting point, incidentally, that in the codification of civil law, the first major step towards the realization of the rule of law, Prussia was a good ten years ahead of France. As for the Polish ruling class, the Prussian administrative and officers' posts were open to them, and numerous Polish nobles – the Radziwills, Radolins, Hutten-Czapskis and Podbielskis, to name but a few – became not only loyal but prominent Prussians for several generations. One of them was to remark sadly after 1871 that the Poles had been able to be Prussians at any time, but could, of course, never be Germans.

This abstract state structure, which was not rooted in any particular nation or tribe but, as it were, was applicable at will, was Prussia's strength. But it could also, as was to emerge presently, become its weakness. It made the state expandable almost without limit – not only capable of conquest but also of genuinely incorporating what had been conquered and drawing new strength from it. But it also made the state dispensable in a particular way to its subjects the moment it failed. It was not only tolerable but in many respects agreeable to become a Prussian subject. So much order, security under the law, or freedom of conscience were not to be found everywhere; there was also a certain pride in being a Prussian. But it was not indispensable, it was not necessary; one was not a Prussian by nature in the sense that one was a Frenchman, an Englishman, a German, a Pole, or even a Bavarian or Saxon. Prussian citizenship was more exchangeable than any other; and if the Prussian state could be pitched over any group of people without particularly upsetting them, rather like a tent, then that tent could also be struck again without this being regarded as a disaster. Prussia was not an organism with innate forces of healing but rather a magnificently constructed state machine – yet only a machine; if the flywheel stopped the machine came to a halt. Under Frederick Wilhelm II's successor the flywheel failed and the machine came to a halt. For several years it seemed as if it could never be started up again.

And yet Prussia did not fall apart. Was it after all something other than a machine? Or could it, perhaps, become something else?

4

THE TEST OF STRENGTH

A Peace-loving King – An Incomprehensible War – Reforms and Clashes about Reforms – Prussia's Westward Displacement

ONCE BEFORE, in the Seven Years' War, Prussia had been subjected to a test of strength. If it had lost that war it would have been carved up in accordance with the plans of the enemy coalition, the way Poland was subsequently carved up, and Prussian history would have been at an end.

Half a century after the Seven Years' War Prussia was again threatened with that fate – indeed twice. After the defeat of 1806 its further existence was in the balance; barely surviving, it risked its life again in 1813. In 1813 too – a circumstance often suppressed in patriotic presentations of history – Prussia's existence hung by a thread for several months. All went well in the end. But Prussia emerged from this double test of strength a changed character, scarcely recognizable.

It was a double test also for another reason: not only because Prussia had twice, in 1806 and in 1813, staked everything, but because – unlike the situation half a century earlier – the external test of strength was accompanied by a domestic one. Not only in its foreign policy did Prussia find itself caught in the crossfire of the great European conflict with Napoleon and the French Revolution, but this crossfire also ran right through domestic politics, and Prussia was fighting for its existence in a state of internal division, pulled one way and another between reform and reaction. In this internal struggle the defeat of 1806-7, which threatened its existence, resulted in temporary victory for the reforming party; the saving War of Liberation of 1813-15, however, led to the triumph of reaction.

Prussian historical myth has always refused to accept this.

According to that myth, which is still firmly rooted in many minds, the twenty years of Prussian history from 1795 to 1815 are divided into two strictly separate periods, periods as black and white as the Prussian flag: the years of the Peace of Basle with revolutionary France, from 1795 to 1806, a period of standstill and decadence, paid for by the collapse of 1806; the period from 1807 to 1812 a period of courageous reforms, regeneration and preparation for the uprising which, as it were according to schedule, took place in 1813 and was rewarded with the victorious Wars of Liberation.

We must put that myth aside. It is not only an oversimplification but a falsification of real history. The entire period in reality was one. The same persons and forces were operative throughout. The two most famous reformist Ministers, Stein and Hardenberg, had been Prussian Ministers well before 1806, and by then the most important military reformer, Scharnhorst, was already Deputy Chief of Staff. The struggle for the modernization of the Prussian state had been going on throughout that time, before 1806 as much as after. Even during the decade of the Peace of Basle Prussia had been eagerly – one might say with touching eagerness – trying to emulate post-revolutionary France in terms of progress and modernity, and to imitate the accomplishments of the French Revolution by reforms from above. The disaster of 1806 helped the reformers to power, more particularly because it so drastically demonstrated the superiority of the new French ideas. No one could have foreseen that there would be anything like 1813. And when the Napoleonic halo evaporated in 1815 the Prussian reforms were also past history.

As early as 1799 the Prussian Minister Struensee (a brother of the famous Struensee who, thirty years earlier, had been active as a reformer in Denmark and paid for it with his young life) said to the French Minister to Berlin:

The salutary Revolution which you effected from the bottom upwards will take place gradually in Prussia from the top downwards. The King is a democrat in his fashion. He is ceaselessly working towards curtailing the privileges of the nobility. . . . In a few years there will be no privileged class left in Prussia.

The wording was perhaps chosen to please his interlocutor but the statement was not a lie. To understand what lay behind it one must realize the following:

Eighteenth-century Prussia had been not only the newest but also the most contemporary state of Europe, strong not through tradition but through modernity. But after the French Revolution there was suddenly a more modern state in existence, with newer and more powerful political ideas. The French 'Liberty, equality, fraternity' carried more fire than the Prussian 'To each his own'.

What is more, it strengthened the state which proclaimed it in a field in which Prussia was especially perceptive: the military field. After all, the French Revolution was not only a political and social revolution but also a military one. France had adopted something entirely novel: general conscription. And during the war years of 1792–95 the Prussians first made the shocking discovery that the French revolutionary armies were lending the war an entirely new dimension, not only by their mass but also by their fighting spirit. The French Revolution had turned the French peasants into soldiers and free landowners at one and the same time; they were now genuinely fighting for 'their' land. Unless Prussia was to be overtaken in the field of its hitherto greatest strength, the military field, something similar had to be made possible also in Prussia, though of course without a revolution: this conclusion had been drawn by the most progressive minds in Prussia as early as 1795. Their thoughts were briefly summed up by Hardenberg after the military disaster of 1806. The ideas of 1789, he said, were irresistible. 'The power of these principles is so great that the state that fails to accept them must inevitably head either towards its own fall or towards their enforced acceptance.' And again: 'Democratic principles in a monarchical government – this seems to me the form appropriate to the spirit of the present age.'

Very well said – but, of course, more easily said than done. What the Prussian reformers had in mind – liberation of the peasants, general conscription, abolition of the class barriers between nobility and bourgeoisie – was more than mere reform, it would have been a revolution from above, and the new king,

Frederick Wilhelm III, though initially entirely open to new ideas, was anything but a revolutionary. He was a very bourgeois, very sober king, exemplary husband to the beautiful, bright and popular Queen Luise, virtuous, adaptable, progressive in a shy and slightly begrudging manner, but also irresolute and at times timidly stubborn. His favourite time, one of his Cabinet Councillors said behind his back, was time to consider.

And opposition was formidable. That the Prussian army, until then undefeated and still wearing the slightly faded laurels of Frederick's wars, opposed any kind of reform was the least of the troubles. Armies are conservative – that appears to be a political law of nature. More serious was the fact that Prussia could not become a second France, even with the best will in the world, because it had, quite simply, a different social structure.

The French Revolution had been a bourgeois revolution, and the French peasantry owed its liberation to a firm class alliance with a powerful, revolutionary, urban property-owning middle class. But in Prussia there was no powerful, self-assured urban property-owning middle class – it simply did not exist. Some 87 per cent of the Prussian population in about 1800 were living in the countryside, in villages and on estates; of the remaining 13 per cent only 6 per cent lived in towns with more than 20,000 inhabitants. And these 6 per cent – all in all barely more than half a million, including errand boys and domestic servants – were, alongside a very modest and almost impecunious merchant class, an educated bourgeoisie of pastors, professors, teachers, artists and, the great majority of them, civil servants. That was not the stuff to make a revolution with, not even a revolution from above.

Admittedly, this educated Prussian middle class flourished during the ten years of the Peace of Basle as it had never done before: Berlin was experiencing an almost hectic flowering of culture, the kind that strangely enough often precedes political disasters. Much the same could have been observed in Paris prior to 1870, in Vienna before 1914 and again in Berlin before 1933. An entire army of literary talent then inhabited the Prussian capital. Aristocrats such as Kleist, Hardenberg (Novalis), Arnim, de la Motte-Fouqué; commoners such as Tieck, Brentano,

Friedrich Schlegel, E. T. A. Hoffman. Romantic Berlin was beginning to outshine classicist Weimar as an intellectual centre. In the salons of Rahel Levin and Dorothea Schlegel the literary and the political worlds mingled. Even a member of the royal family, the brilliant and eccentric Prince Louis Ferdinand, was a frequent visitor there, and in the entourage of the King himself a number of untitled Cabinet Councillors now called the tune – the 'Prussian Jacobines' Beyme, Lombard and Mencken (the last, incidentally, was Bismarck's maternal grandfather). Among the aristocratic Ministers and diplomats there were many, such as Hardenberg and Humboldt, who felt closer to the new middle-class political-literary intelligentsia than to their own peers, the country Junkers. Certainly no ossification or immobility; on the contrary, a brilliant, witty world buzzing with modern progressive, humane and reformist ideas. One officer, the subsequent army reformer Boyen, already publicly recommended the abolition of the whip and the rod in the army, and there was universal talk of liberation of the peasantry, free trade, emancipation of the Jews, and city self-government.

Not only in the salons. Most of the reforms subsequently implemented by Stein and Hardenberg between 1806 and 1813 had been planned and prepared in the Ministries well before 1806, but they had not been put into effect. Essentially reforms remained an issue in the capital, among intellectuals and senior civil servants. In the countryside, where 87 per cent of Prussian subjects lived and where the Junkers ruled, reforms remained taboo, for the moment, in the face of massive resistance from a still totally intact and robustly sound feudal system. One might say that Prussia was unable to imitate the French Revolution – even though its best brains thought it to be necessary – because it was too healthy for it. In Prussia around the year 1800 there was no 'revolutionary situation' of the kind that had existed in France ten years earlier. There feudalism had gradually decayed in the eighteenth century. In Prussia it was still entirely robust and viable, and did not even have to try particularly hard to dismiss the reform plans of the capital as idle chatter.

Only one major reform was accomplished before 1806 – the

liberation of the peasants on state domains. This, admittedly, was far more successful than Stein's later attempt to liberate the peasants on private estates. Where the state itself was the land-lord it was able not only to plan and discuss but also to act. Over 50,000 domain peasants became free owners prior to 1806 – a greater number than throughout the whole period from 1807 to 1848. Otherwise it was just a matter of plans and drafts; there was a pro-reform atmosphere, but as yet there was no reform policy. There was no lack of open-mindedness or readiness for progress in the Prussia of the Peace of Basle – but the country somehow remained incapable of movement and fettered to its ancient institutions. These fetters were only broken by external defeat; but that, simultaneously, very nearly broke up the entire state.

The circumstances which led to the war and to the defeat of 1806 make a strange and instructive story. King Frederick Wilhelm III, in marked contrast to his two predecessors, was a genuine pacifist. Shortly before his accession he had, for his own instruction and guidance, written down some 'Thoughts on the Art of Government'. There we read:

> The greatest happiness of a country consists reliably in lasting peace; the best policy, therefore, is that which always has this principle before its eyes, if our neighbours will leave us in peace. One should never interfere in the quarrels of others which do not concern one ... and in order not to be involved in other people's quarrels against one's will one should avoid alliances which sooner or later might thus involve us.

In other words, peace through neutrality; and throughout nine years Frederick Wilhelm stuck to that principle, apparently with success.

These nine years were nearly all of them war years in Europe, but the country which under Frederick Wilhelm's two pre-decessors had been acting on the principle 'that nothing could happen on the continent that did not concern Prussia, and that no political event of any importance should take place without its participation', now persevered in its self-chosen isolation and remained an island of peace. It even profited from it: during the great West German consolidation under French auspices, the so-called Reich Deputation Resolution of 1803, Prussia once more gained a substantial piece of territory, virtually the whole of Westphalia. Entirely without war. What more could anyone want? And a year later, when Napoleon made himself Emperor of the French and the German Emperor Francis, with a premonition of things to come, assumed the title of 'Emperor of Austria', Napoleon even invited the King of Prussia to adopt an imperial title as well: Emperor of Prussia. But Frederick Wilhelm III modestly declined. 'One should not allow oneself to be blinded by any seeming glory to be won', he had written in his above-quoted 'Thoughts on the Art of Government'. He did not wish to place Prussia in the same class as the four empires and possibly be involved in their quarrels. He wanted to remain a simple king of Prussia, and above all he wanted to be left in peace. If there was to be war then he did not wish to be responsible.

The Minister of one of the small central German states, which were then living under the protection of Prussian neutrality, Goethe, commented on all this with worldly-wise scepticism, as though shaking his head:

Although the world was aflame at all corners and ends, although Europe had assumed another shape, cities and navies were being shattered on land and on sea, yet central and northern Germany were still enjoying a certain feverish peace amidst which we were indulging in a problematical security. The great Empire in the west had been founded, it was sending out roots and shoots in all directions. Meanwhile Prussia seemed to enjoy the privilege of consolidating itself in the north.

One can hear the disbelief. Goethe did not trust the Prussian peace. He was a more realistic statesman than Frederick Wilhelm III.

What Frederick Wilhelm failed to realize was that neutrality changes its character when the surrounding power relations are changed. When Prussia in 1795 concluded its separate Peace of Basle with France, the French Republic was still a hard-pressed state, happy to buy Prussia's neutrality and willing to pay a high price for it. Ten years later the French Empire had become the strongest power in Europe, about to assume hegemony over the entire continent. Unnoticed, Prussia's neutrality had been transformed into passive partisanship for France. In 1805 Austria and Russia formed an alliance with Britain in order to break Napoleon's supremacy. The moment had come to stand up and be counted. Russia and Austria were pressing Prussia to join the alliance. But Frederick Wilhelm continued to cling to his neutrality. The most that he allowed himself to be persuaded to by the Tsar in Potsdam in 1805, at a solemn and somewhat theatrical fraternization scene by the coffin of Frederick the Great, was armed mediation. But for that Napoleon was too swift. Before he even received the Prussian emissary he defeated the Austrians and Russians at Austerlitz and forced the Austrians to conclude a separate peace. Russia grudgingly withdrew behind its frontiers. There was nothing left for Prussia to mediate.

Instead Napoleon now offered Prussia an alliance – or rather, he demanded it imperiously. And in February 1806 – a fact often hushed up – very much against the inclination of the King, that alliance actually came into being, though only against Britain and not against Russia. Prussia's neutrality had even in the 1805 war amounted to favouring the stronger side, the French. After the French victory Prussia was glad enough to find Napoleon paying for it with an offer of an alliance and rewarding it by territorial aggrandisement. Prussia was allowed to take British Hanover; it did so in June. Britain replied with the seizure of all Prussian merchant ships. Prussia, hardly knowing how all this had come about, found itself on the side of France and at war with Britain. And then, a mere three months later, the war against Britain suddenly became a war against France.

How did that happen? The turnabout seemed inexplicable. No one had wanted or planned that war, not even Napoleon. He still viewed the Prussian army with respect – 'if he were still alive we should not be here,' he said at Frederick the Great's grave which he visited after his victory – and in 1806 he still preferred to make Prussia his junior partner rather than having to defeat and conquer it. As for Frederick Wilhelm, he was love of peace personified. Indeed, one might say that he had stumbled into the war from offended love of peace. He had not forgiven Napoleon for having forced him into the alliance. He was offended also by the disdain with which French troops had already marched uninvited through Prussian territory at Ansbach. If he had to make war, then he would rather make it against him who had offended him, against him who 'would not leave him in peace', than against Britain which had done him no harm. Besides, the King realized that, once allied to Napoleon, he would not in the long run be able to escape war against his friend, the Tsar. In July Prussia concluded a kind of re-insurance treaty with the Tsar, behind the back of his new French ally. Napoleon learnt about it and replied with a menacing deployment in Thuringia. Thereupon Prussia mobilized and, by way of an ultimatum, demanded that this concentration of troops be stopped. Napoleon's response was invasion. Mistrust on the French side, irritation on the Prussian side, offended vanity on both sides – a row among allies, and then a short circuit. Neither side had any clear plans about what it wanted to achieve by this war; on the Prussian side, moreover, there had been absolutely no assessment of its prospects. Without allies and without political objective Prussia conducted the war of an affronted man of honour; one might almost say that Prussia in 1806 was still defending its long-lost neutrality. What a contrast to the Prussian wars of the eighteenth century!

One single day brought the military decision. On 14 October 1806 the two Prussian armies, marching separately, were separately defeated in the battles of Jena and Auerstedt (they were two separate battles and not, as is always asserted, a 'double battle'). That was not really a surprise: at that time Napoleon had won every battle against any opponent. What was surprising was what followed: the total lack of opposition, indeed the eagerness with which the decision of Jena and Auerstedt was accepted in Prussia; the swift capitulation of the defeated but by no means annihilated armies, the unresisting surrender of fortresses, the King's flight to East Prussia, the almost jubilant welcome for the victor in Berlin, the ready 'collaboration' of the entire state apparatus with the victor; the Prussian civil servants who even took a kind of oath of loyalty to Napoleon. Again what a contrast to Prussian imperturbable steadfastness in the Seven Years' War, after its equally heavy defeat at Kunersdorf!

That contrast calls for an explanation, as does the earlier outbreak of the war. Perhaps the explanation is the same. The war of 1806 had been a short-circuit action. Nobody quite understood it: everything was happening in a rush. No one had time to understand why Prussia and France, friends for the past ten years and recently allies, should suddenly be enemies. Everything seemed like an incomprehensible misunderstanding – and Napoleon's swift victory like its clarification. Now one would get on together again, and everything would be as before.

In actual fact nothing was as before, and the life-and-death crisis of the Prussian state was yet to begin. Its destiny was solely in the hands of the victor; and Napoleon was doubly disappointed in Prussia: he had wished to have it as an ally and he had imagined it to be much stronger than it had proved to be. Anger and contempt now determined his policy; Prussia had to be punished and at the same time it might be used as a counter in the political game. Beyond that Napoleon had no clear plans for Prussia. He was improvising. His first concept was a halved Prussia as a buffer state and barrier against Russia: he would incorporate Prussia's West German territories into his Confederation of the Rhine; between the Elbe and the Bug Prussia might be allowed, for the moment, to continue to exist as a now purely Eastern, semi-Polish state. A preliminary peace was in fact concluded on that basis in Charlottenburg on 30 October. But then Napoleon came up with additional demands: a break with Russia and unrestricted right of transit for the French armies. After all, the war with Russia, dormant since Austerlitz, was not yet concluded. Now Frederick Wilhelm objected, after unnerving discussions with his Ministers at Osterode in East Prussia, where he had fled. So Napoleon, angry and impatient, devised a plan for Prussia's total dissolution: Silesia to be returned to Austria, Poland to be restituted, the Hohenzollern dynasty to be dethroned. It is significant that he could seriously conceive such a plan; he never thought up anything of the kind for Austria although he had fought many more and much longer wars against that country. But one could think of Europe without Prussia.

Subsequently Napoleon dropped the idea again. The fate of Prussia now depended, also for him, on the outcome of his war with Russia. He set his armies marching towards East Prussia. Meanwhile the Russians had also moved in, and the Prussians, too, scraped together an army corps. On 18 February 1807 the atrociously bloody winter battle of Eylau was fought, the first one which Napoleon did not win. The armies disengaged without a decision, and the allies drew courage once more. In April a formal Russian-Prussian alliance was concluded which in substance anticipated the later alliance of 1813 : war until Napoleon's complete overthrow, no separate peace, restoration of Prussia within its frontiers of 1805. But that for the moment remained a dream.

In June Napoleon again won a clear victory over the Russians, the Tsar's generals urgently advised an armistice, and Napoleon himself was not yet ready in 1807 for a campaign in Russia. Thus a dramatic conciliation meeting between the French Emperor and the Russian Tsar was held on a raft in the middle of the Niemen and this was followed by the Peace of Tilsit. This also decided the fate of Prussia. It was no longer consulted on the matter.

However, with its Russian alliance and its token resistance in East Prussia, Prussia had at least made sure that its future would no longer lie in Napoleon's hands alone but in two pairs of hands : those of Napoleon and of the Tsar Alexander. It was not much of a gain for Prussia. The Tsar grandly brushed aside his treaty of alliance of April and the obligation of restoring the Prussia of 1805; what did he care about a half-dead Prussia anyway. However, he owed it to his honour to preserve his small Prussian ally from total extinction, and Napoleon for his part was prepared to accept this without much opposition. A deal was struck : each of the two high contracting parties maintained, as it were, a pawn on the other party's chessboard. France's pawn was Prussian Poland; this was set up as the Duchy of Warsaw from the territories which Prussia had acquired at the last partition of Poland

and assigned to the Kingdom of Saxony – which in practice meant the Confederation of the Rhine. Russia, for its part, acquired, as a barrier, a Prussia reduced to its 1772 frontiers; this was not assigned to the Confederation of the Rhine but maintained a nominal independence for which it had to thank the Tsar. However, it remained French-occupied territory; to that extent the Tsar made the worse bargain, but that was in line with the power ratio. Prussia willy-nilly had to fit in with the compromise of the two great powers. Its existence as a state, even though paltry, had just barely been saved.

Yet in this impoverished and humiliated Prussia all the great reform plans, which prior to the disaster had been just plans, were now carried out, hard upon each other: the liberation of the peasantry, self-administration for the cities, opening up of the officers' corps to commoners, equal rights for nobility and bourgeoisie with regard to land ownership, equal civil rights for the Jews, free pursuit of trades, the new French military system, abolition of corporal punishment in the army – in short, the entire social programme of the French Revolution. But the social programme only – not the political programme: no people's sovereignty, no parliament, and, of course, no republic. The King of Prussia had no intention of abdicating. His state was merely to be strengthened by being placed on broader foundations, and for that purpose the conquered adopted the victorious system of the conqueror: 'democratic principles in a monarchist government', as Hardenberg had formulated it.

The revolution from above, much talked of in the past, was now taking place. Having only just escaped with its bare life, reduced to less than half its size, Prussia nevertheless found the strength for an internal renewal. That was a tremendous achievement and proof that there was life in the state yet. In an entirely different way from the time of the Seven Years' War, but possibly even more strikingly, Prussia proved its strength in misfortune. Then it had hung on with gritted teeth; this time one might almost say that it had risen from the dead.

Almost. With all respect for the will to live and the strength of renewal which manifested themselves in the reforms of the years 1807 to 1812, one is bound to observe soberly that many of them at first remained on paper.

Nor should one disregard another aspect: the reforms, and more particularly the liberation of the peasantry, by no means united the country but divided it. After all, Prussia was not only a state ruled by a king but also still a state run by the Junkers, and Stein's Edict on the emancipation of the peasantry was virtually a declaration of war on the Junkers; like Frederick Wilhelm I, Stein was out to 'destroy the authority of the Junkers'. But the Junkers had not let their authority be destroyed that easily in the past, nor would they now.

The nobility established a powerful opposition against the reforms. Its spokesman, Friedrich Ludwig von der Marwitz, a remarkable figure, wrote: 'Stein started to revolutionize the fatherland, he opened the war of the property-less against property, of industry against agriculture, of the mobile against the stable'; and when Stein, the 'foreigner from Nassau', was dismissed in 1808, another Old Prussian, General Yorck, the man who five years later was to sound the signal for the War of Liberation, wrote: 'One head full of nonsense is now crushed; the rest of the viper's brood will dissolve in its own venom.' That was the extent of the bitterness with which reformers and anti-reformers were facing each other in Prussia at the time. Two years later Hardenberg had Marwitz put under detention for high treason. But in 1813 Marwitz, too, hastened to arms, as the leader of a mounted *Landwehr* company of 'his' peasants whom he equipped at his own expense and personally drilled and commanded. The opponents of reform were not lacking in Prussian patriotism either.

Moreover the reformers were divided among themselves – a subtle division, at first seemingly only a difference of nuance, a hair crack which subsequently widened into an abyss. The ones were simply Prussian patriots; the others were then beginning, sometimes still unconsciously, to become nationalists, and, what is more, German nationalists: after all, there was no such thing as a Prussian nation. The distinction is best understood if one looks more closely at the two great reform Ministers, Stein and Hardenberg.

Both of them were Prussians by choice, from the German West: Stein from Hesse, Hardenberg from Hanover. But whereas Hardenberg devoted his entire life to Prussia's service, Stein really only gave a guest performance. 'I have but one fatherland, its name is Germany', he wrote after his dismissal, and in the same letter added more sharply: 'If Austria can become the master of a united Germany I will glady put Prussia at its disposal.' Hardenberg would never have written such a thing; to him Prussia was never at anyone's disposal. This differentiated the two men also in their foreign policy: Stein was always ready to sacrifice Prussia's existence to his hatred of France. If he had had his way Prussia would have struck out again in 1808 and 1809, from a totally hopeless position, trying to unleash an all-German popular war as in Spain or in the Tyrol. Hardenberg utterly rejected this idea: it would quite certainly have cost Prussia's existence. Even he, in 1813, acted with considerable boldness – but at least he waited until there was a small prospect of success. Until then he pursued a policy of adaptation.

Unquestionably Hardenberg was the better politician of the two. Stein, a character somewhere between Martin Luther and Michael Kohlhaas, always wanted to crash through walls head-on, and on the whole was a failure as a politician. After his second dismissal in 1808 (he had once before resigned his post in anger in 1806) he never again became a Prussian Minister. (He subsequently entered Russian service in the war against Napoleon, but there he did not get very far either and from 1815 onwards lived on his ancestral estate in Nassau as an embittered private person.) Hardenberg, much more skilful and flexible, and in his private life not a puritan like Stein but a man of the world, a cavalier and charmer like Metternich and Talleyrand, in 1810, in the post of 'State Chancellor' attained a position such as no one had held in Prussia before him and only Bismarck after him; he kept it until his death in 1822. In the decisive crisis of 1813 it was he, far more than the King, who in practice made Prussian politics.

To return to the rift within the reform party, as personified by Stein and Hardenberg. The early German nationalists who then emerged in Prussia included some names which became famous in German cultural history: the poets Heinrich von Kleist and Ernst Moritz Arndt, the philosopher Fichte ('Speeches to the German Nation'), the theologian Schleiermacher, the General Gneisenau; even the somewhat ludicrous 'Father of Gymnastics' Jahn was not denied posterity's fame. They personified something that in the later nineteenth century was to become a massive political force; precursors of the German national movement, they have gone down in German national historiography as heroes. But this should not blind us to the fact that in their own day they were outsiders, with a following, if any, among university students, and without any real influence on actual Prussian politics. To ascribe to them and their views the decision to make war in 1813 – as has often been done since – is a doctoring of history. Instead the first real move towards the war came from a man of diametrically opposite views, the Old Prussian diehard and anti-reformer General Yorck. And the war itself was by no means a revolutionary people's war but an entirely disciplined state war, one might even say a cabinet war. The assertions of Theodor Körner's verses 'This is no war of which the Crowns have knowledge'; 'The people rise, the storm breaks loose' – may have been 'good poetry' (as the King once said of Gneisenau's ideas of a people's war) but they do not represent historical truth.

Nor is it historical truth that, throughout the period from 1807 to 1813, Prussia had been, as it were, feverishly expecting Liberation, or that it had been the purpose, or at least the effect, of the reforms to win the people over for a War of Liberation. The purpose of the reforms, if anything, was to make the best of defeat by adjusting to it; what gradually made the whole population once more ready for war was something totally different: the worsening material hardships caused by French occupation and the exorbitant reparation payments which Napoleon exacted from the defeated country. In Napoleon's eyes Prussia was still a defeated enemy, one who had criminally rejected the opportunity of becoming an ally; it was therefore deliberately treated with harshness, becoming something like the whipping boy of Napoleonic Europe. Prussian everyday life during the French period was characterized far less by the reforms or the quarrel about the reforms than by naked economic plight.

In order to raise the 120 million francs of war reparations, a gigantic sum at the time but implacably exacted by Napoleon, domains had to be sold, usurious loans taken up, taxes increased; even something as unprecedented as a graduated income tax (from 10 to 30 per cent) had to be imposed on the Prussians for a time. Meanwhile Napoleon's Continental Blockade – a ban on all overseas trade, designed to hit Britain – was paralysing the economy and sea-borne trade, causing widespread bankruptcies and unemployment. Naturally this gave rise to bitterness and, far more than the reforms, helped to make the Prussian man in the street in 1813 more grimly ready for war than he had been in 1806. The war of 1813 was popular while that of 1806 had not been – but this does not mean that it was a people's war. Moreover, it had been unpredictable to the very last moment – who could suspect until 1812 that the powers who had peacefully shared out Europe between them at Tilsit would again make war, and who, before the winter of 1812–13, would have thought that this war would bring military disaster to Napoleon? Until then Prussia had to fit itself as well as it could into Napoleonic Europe, and it did so, gritting its teeth, without feeling sorry for itself, with a certain sober toughness in accepting conditions, and even with a certain readiness to adapt itself, a readiness expressed in the reforms.

It is by no means easy to reduce the atmosphere of the reformist Prussia of the French era to a common denominator. Hardships, oppression, reversion to poor conditions, patriotic bitterness on the one side; and on the other a sense of lucky survival, pleasure in innovation, and even hope – by no means necessarily just hope of a war of liberation. 'Prussia must offset by spiritual strength what it has lost in physical strength', the Minister of Culture, Humboldt, declared when he founded the University of Berlin in 1810. That did not sound warlike. In many respects post-1806

Berlin was still the same Berlin as in the years of the Peace of Basle. The same literary-political salons continued to flourish, the same romantic poets still wrote their poetry. Not even attitudes to the French were as uniformly or unambiguously hostile as patriotic legend subsequently depicted them. Theodor Fontane, though born later, was still able, on his rambles through the Mark Brandenburg, to question surviving witnesses, paints a far more differentiated picture of the age in his novel *Before the Storm*, set in the winter of 1812–13. There he describes how, as late as January 1813, a Saxon officer returning injured from the Russian campaign, reads his notes on the Battle of Borodino to a Berlin literary circle with great applause, although French army leaders play heroic parts in the account. Fontane continues:

Conditions in Prussia then [as late as the beginning of 1813], and especially in its capital, were so peculiar that such a predeliction could be voiced without the least concern of giving offence. No one knew where he should stand politically, or scarcely even in his heart, for while just before the outbreak of the war three hundred of our best officers had entered Russian service in order not to have to fight for the 'hereditary enemy', they were faced in the Auxiliary Corps, which we had to raise for just that 'hereditary enemy', by their brothers and relations in equal or double numbers. We considered ourselves essentially spectators, clearly realizing all the advantages that were bound to stem from a Russian victory and therefore desiring that victory, but we were far from identifying with Kutuzov or Vorontsov to such an extent that an account of French military superiority, in which we willy-nilly played a part, might offend us in any way whatsoever.

At the beginning of 1812, before the outbreak of the war with Russia, Napoleon had in fact for the second time forced an alliance upon Prussia – 'forced' in the eyes of Prussia which would have preferred to remain a spectator; in Napoleon's eyes he had given Prussia a chance of making up for its breach of alliance in 1806 and enabling it – now that, as it were, it had served its sentence – to be graciously accepted after all as a junior partner. It was pure chance that in the Russian war of 1812 Yorck's corps was deployed only to protect the army's flank in the Baltic area and thereby escaped the disaster of the Grande Armée on its retreat from

Moscow. As is known, Yorck, after that disaster, on 31 December 1812, agreed with the Russian General Diebitsch at Tauroggen, over the head of King and Government, to opt out of the French war. He certainly did not change allegiance to the Russians then. Shortly afterwards, when Stein, now a Russian Commissar, appeared at Yorck's headquarters and demanded a clear-cut switch of allegiance, the two diehards snarled at each other with fur bristling like a couple of tomcats. Yorck quite resolutely refused to go beyond a military neutralization of his corps (and of East Prussia protected by that corps); it was up to the King to decide on peace or war. Stein threatened that in that case he would use Russian force of arms. Yorck, in turn, threatened that he would sound a general attack and then Stein might see what would become of him and his Russians. That scene was not included in any Prussian school primer afterwards.

The decision on peace or war was in fact not made in East Prussia. It was made by the King, but he made it very hesitantly and reluctantly. Frederick Wilhelm, not fond of adventures at the best of times, was now once bitten. He could still feel the lesson of 1807 in his bones. Then, too, he had an alliance with the Tsar but the Tsar had unconcernedly brushed it aside at Tilsit, when it no longer fitted into his game. Frederick Wilhelm was not going to be had a second time. Besides, he did not really trust Russian military superiority. Just as he had stubbornly clung to the idea of neutrality so he now did to the principle 'No move against Napoleon without a firm alliance with Russia *and Austria*'. But Austria, as indeed Prussia, was still officially allied with Napoleon. General von dem Knesebeck, who was eventually despatched to Russian headquarters at Kalisch towards the end of February 1813, at first only had instructions to mediate an armistice.

But it turned into a treaty of alliance all the same. Probably Knesebeck had contingency instructions to conclude that alliance if the Russians would not settle for mediation; it is not even entirely certain that the King had expressly authorized such contingency instructions. Certainly their spiritual author was not the King but Hardenberg. Hardenberg, coolly calculating, regarded the Russian alliance – now that Prussia was, in any case, becoming a theatre of war – not only as the better chance but also as the lesser risk than continuation of the French alliance. After the annihilation of the Grande Armée the Russians now seemed clearly the stronger side to him.

This the King doubted. He insisted that Napoleon was still the stronger so long as he was facing Russia and Prussia alone, and that only a triple alliance of Russia, Prussia and Austria could be a match for him. He was to be proved right. The spring campaign of 1813 went badly, the allied Prussians and Russians lost two battles, and when an armistice was concluded in June the alliance was again creaking at the joints. The Tsar's advisers felt after the defeats of Lützen and Bautzen that one should now abide by the successful self-defence, that the Treaty of Tilsit should be renewed, and that Russia should withdraw behind its own frontiers. If that had happened Prussia would have been lost. Napoleon would certainly not have forgiven the second defection. In the summer of 1813 Prussia was hovering between life and death. But there was one glimmer of hope left.

That glimmer of hope was that Austria used the armistice for armed mediation. But the Franco-Austrian negotiations in Dresden and the Peace Congress which followed in Prague brought Prussia once more into deadly danger. The reason was that Napoleon there offered to the Austrian negotiator Metternich a universal peace at the expense of Prussia: Silesia to be returned to Austria, Poland to be restituted with West Prussia, East Prussia to go to Russia, and Brandenburg complete with the capital Berlin to go to Saxony. Everyone would carry away some profit from the war, and only of Prussia nothing would be left. From Napoleon's point of view it was entirely understandable that he should now wish to wipe out Prussia, which had twice betrayed him; and the offer of the return of Silesia must have been a serious temptation to Austria. It is to Metternich's credit that he did not swallow the bait. Metternich did not think in narrowly Austrian terms; what he wanted was the restoration of a European balance of power. And that, in his view, demanded a Prussian factor; above all it demanded France's withdrawal beyond the

Rhine. But that Napoleon was not prepared to concede, and thus the negotiations failed. Austria now joined the war on the side of Russia and Prussia, and that decided the outcome. At Leipzig, in the four-day 'Battle of the Nations' from 16 to 19 October, Napoleon's generalship was overcome by the superior power of the allies. The King of Prussia had been proved right: what the forces of Russia and Prussia had failed to achieve, had been achieved by Austria's accession. Napoleon's power was broken. Leipzig had decided the war. The campaign in France in 1814 and, even more so, the brief Belgian campaign of 1815 following Napoleon's short-lived return to the French throne, were no more than an epilogue.

We have dealt here very briefly with the Wars of Liberation, about which, of course, one might write an entire book – many in fact have been written about them – and we have done so with good reason. Our subject is Prussia, and the Wars of Liberation were not Prussian wars in the sense that the wars of Frederick the Great and those of his successor had been. They were the final act in a more than twenty years' war of Europe against the French Revolution and of Napoleon against Europe, and in that war Prussia had played only a secondary role. The real protagonists against France had been Austria, Russia and, above all, Britain. They all had fought much longer, much more often and much more decisively than Prussia. Most of the time Prussia had been neutral, and twice, briefly, it had actually been allied to France; its strange intermezzo appearance of 1806–7 had ended disastrously, and only in the final act had it played a useful – though still by no means the main – role. True, it had staked its existence, it had fought bravely, and it had somewhat restored its military reputation after its battering in 1806 – but to the victorious principal powers Prussia was only a late arrival and co-victor, one which had only at the last minute made its modest contribution to the common cause. At the Congress of Vienna for the reorganization of Europe, which drew the new frontiers in 1814–15 – frontiers which lasted for roughly half a century – Prussia played second fiddle: outwardly ranking equal and enjoying equal respect with the four great powers – Russia, Austria, Britain and France –

it remained in effect the object of their policy rather than a co-creator. It was allowed to speak, and it was universally conceded that it should again occupy a similar position to that before the misfortune of 1806. But how and where was decided by others.

The shortlived Prussian-Russian treaty of alliance of 1807 had still clearly envisaged the restoration of Prussia 'within its 1805 frontiers'; that of 1813 merely spoke of 'on a similar scale and in equal strength as in 1806'. Russia now was no longer prepared to leave the Polish heartlands to Prussia; it wanted Poland for itself. Only West Prussia and Posen were allowed to remain part of Prussia in order to give it a coherent territory and a tolerable eastern frontier. As compensation for the lost Polish territory Prussia demanded Saxony, the ancient object of Frederick the Great's dreams, and Russia had no objection. But Austria had not forgotten the Seven Years' War which had begun with Frederick's attempted annexation of Saxony. It resolutely opposed Saxony's surrender to Prussia and for a while it looked as if the alliance might break up, and the Congress of Vienna fail, over this issue. Then Prussia gave in. It no longer felt strong enough to assert its claim to Saxony and perhaps even lacked the determination to do so. The conviction that its existence could only be assured in a firm triple alliance with Russia and Austria had become the state's official maxim in 1813 and remained so for a whole generation; all other interests were subordinated to it.

Thus Prussia received its compensation for its Polish losses in a place where it had never expected it and where indeed it was not all that welcome: in the Rhineland. The frontier which had to be defended there was still regarded as threatened; the 'Watch on the Rhine' was not an enviable task. The population which now fell to Prussia was as un-Prussian as possible – middle-class, urban, Catholic, long accustomed to ecclesiastic and more recently to French rule. The British historian A. J. P. Taylor has called this compensation by annexation of the Rhineland a kind of practical joke played on poor Prussia by the great powers. That Germany's greatest coalfield was situated there and that it would one day become the biggest German industrial region no one could then surmise.

Prussia emerged from the Congress of Vienna in a strangely transformed territorial shape, consisting of two unconnected masses of territory in the East and the West, which on the map, rather like God the Father and Adam on Michelangelo's famous ceiling of the Sistine Chapel, were stretching out their index fingers towards one another without touching. That strangely divided state body very appropriately symbolized Prussia's not quite successful restoration, the semi-defeat which still hung over it, the two-edged success with which it had come out of the great Napoleonic crisis in spite of 1813–15. It was now, praise the Lord, once more a moderately important, moderately secure state, but it was no longer the old Prussia, no longer the boldly independent, adventurous, freely operating small great power it used to be. It was embedded in a European system and depending on others, stronger than itself, from whom it dared not detach itself and who actually prescribed its territory – prescribed it differently from the way Prussia would have chosen for itself. The wild horse had been tamed and was now marching in harness.

5

THE THREE BLACK EAGLES

A Different Prussia – Consolidation and Reaction – Prussia's German Union – The Capitulation of Olmütz

THE PRUSSIA which presented itself to the world in the decade following 1815 was a different Prussia. Eighteenth-century Prussia had been progressive, pugnacious and free-thinking, a state of the Enlightenment. Prussia between the ages of Napoleon and Bismarck was reactionary, peaceful, emphatically Christian, a state of romanticism.

In fact, the age that was dawning was generally romantic and reactionary, and to that extent Prussia remained true to itself in being – as it had always been – in step with its age. And it remained the old Prussia in the sense that it not only kept in line with its age but positively marched in step with it – with precision, like a company on the parade ground, beginning with a precisely performed about-face.

The Prussia of the turn of the century had been about to copy the French Revolution, though from the top downwards, and the defeated Prussia of the years between 1806 and 1813 had actually been serious about it in many fields. Admittedly, as we have seen, the reforms even then had come up against bitter domestic reaction, and the victory over Napoleon had simultaneously been a victory of that reaction.

This should be clearly understood. Domestic and foreign policy were not to be neatly separated in that great European crisis. Until 1813 Prussia had tried to remain neutral; twice, for a short time, willingly or not, it had even been allied to France. It was in line with such an attitude that, in its own way, it should accept the modern French ideas and transform them into a policy of reform. But now, at the decisive last moment, it had joined the anti-French coalition of the old powers and, on their side, been victorious; and that victory now took the wind out of the sails of the reform party. While France had been victorious, its ideas, too, seemed irresistible; following the victory of the old powers, to whom Prussia now belonged, these old ideas had again gained the upper hand. Events seemed to have proved them stronger. After all, even France hastened to bring back the Bourbons. Prussia had no need to restore its Hohenzollerns, but it no longer wished to think about reforms.

It is quite surprising that it did not immediately abolish most of them. Only the emancipation of the peasantry, which had not gone at all well right from the start, was largely revoked in 1816. But the new urban order and freedom for trade were maintained; and so – at least on paper – was the equality before the law of bourgeoisie and nobility, as well as equal rights for the Jews. The new military constitution of universal conscription was not even formally put into effect until 1814; during the period of occupation it had only been possible to practice it secretly. In the years which followed there was also a thorough-going reorganization of the state territory and state administration, the establishment of a state church and a State Council; even the idea of a 'representation of the people', held out by the King in 1815, was toyed with for a number of years before it was finally dropped in 1819. In 1818 internal tariffs were abolished, and provincial 'estates' and provincial Diets were instituted.

Hans-Joachim Schoeps, the apologist of the 'other Prussia' of the restoration period, speaks of a 'pre-constitutional' state which Prussia was then establishing; and this term is acceptable. Compared with the monarchist absolutism of the eighteenth century the institutionally structured Prussian civil service state after 1815, with its clear division of competences, begins to look like a constitutional state; except, of course, as a Rhenish Liberal put it in 1818, that among the numerous state institutions regulating the performance of the monarch's powers there was none 'in which the ruler is eye to eye with the nation. Nothing great faces him.'

Nevertheless the organization of the Prussian state, in the shape which it adopted during the years from 1814 to 1819, the years of consolidation and 'counter-reform', and which it was to maintain for a hundred years – in its systematic character, tidiness and clear structure – had an impressive appearance. At the centre, as the ultimate instance of decision, there was still the King, but now surrounded by a responsible Ministry and a State Council, a kind of House of Nobles, in which the royal princes, the Ministers, the Chief Presidents of the Provinces, the Corps commanders and thirty-four members appointed by the King had a voice in legislation. In addition there were ten (subsequently, through partial fusion, eight) Provinces headed by a Chief President, divided into Government Districts, sub-divided in their turn into Areas; in each Province an advisory Provincial Diet consisting of three 'estates': nobility, bourgeoisie and peasantry. As a parallel set-up, but independent and likewise structured in three tiers, was the judiciary: Local Courts, Land Courts, Superior Courts. Also independent and again as a parallel structure were the armed forces: in each Province a Corps under the command of a general, in each Government District a division, in each Area a regiment. And in addition, as another parallel structure, was a national Church with General Superintendents corresponding to Chief Presidents, and Superintendents corresponding to the Government Presidents.

This last point calls for further examination – after all, it is something entirely new in Prussian history. Classical Prussia in the eighteenth century had been a decidedly secular state, a state of the Englightenment, tolerant, indeed indifferent, towards all religions. The Prussia of the restoration period wanted to become a Christian state, it was 'officially' devout, and it gave itself even something like a national Church – the 'Prussian Union', through which the King, as Supreme Bishop, forced the Calvinist and Lutheran denominations into a common Church organization. In spite of keeping their separate Creeds they had to form a joint Church organization with joint ecclesiastical authorities, a common personnel of pastors, joint spiritual supervisory authorities and a common order of divine service; the last issue, known as the '*Agende*', gave rise to unending quarrels in which the King often himself intervened as a mediator. There was also, for the first time, a serious clash with the Catholic Church in the newly-Prussian Rhineland, mainly because of its opposition to mixed marriages. The King was in favour of mixed marriages. What he would have liked best would have been an ecumenical system, a universal Christian Church within which the different denominations would represent no more than, in a manner of speaking, provinces of faith. He, too, favoured toleration, but no longer in the style of Frederick from religious indifference but a kind of brotherly toleration based on an all-Christian religious fervour.

Behind this new official piety there was a good deal of politics – Christianity as a state ideology – but also a fair amount of romanticism. German romanticism, centred – not by accident – on Berlin ever since the turn of the century, was not only a literary movement but also a political ideology: the counter-ideology to Enlightenment, a return to the forces of sentiment against the claims of reason. The French Revolution had chosen ancient Rome as its model – at first republican Rome and then imperial Rome. The restoration powers, endeavouring to overcome revolution, tried to use romanticism to revive the Middle Ages: Christian kingship, chivalry, the feudal values of loyalty and vassalage. None of the three allied powers did this with greater enthusiasm than Prussia, which had not experienced any Middle Ages but was, in a sense, now trying to catch up with them. Heine saw this only as a revolting piece of hypocrisy:

I did not trust Prussia, that tall sham-pious Knight in spats, with his big belly and wide-open trap, with that corporal's stick which he first dips in Holy Water before hitting out with it. I disliked that philosophically-Christian army spirit, that hotchpotch of small beer, lies and sand. Distasteful, profoundly distasteful, this Prussia was to me – this stiff, hypocritical and sham-holy Prussia, that Tartuffe among states.

It cannot be denied that the convert's zeal of this lately

converted state did have something extreme, something unsound, about it. A perfectly constructed state machine, animated – as it were artificially inspired – by a romantic dream of medieval Christianity: military bands starting their great tattoo with the chorale 'I pray unto the power of love'. It certainly was odd.

But the charge of mere hypocrisy and sham-piety is nevertheless a little superficial. The new Prussian piety was an assumed piety, but it was intended seriously. There was not only the slightly artificial, slightly enforced new state Church of the 'Prussian Union', there was also an entirely unofficial, spontaneous, profoundly emotional movement of pietist resurgence which in the thirties and forties turned numerous Pomeranian estates into private houses of prayer and penitence. It is impossible to describe as hypocritical such evidence of romantic piety as the paintings of the Pomeranian Caspar David Friedrich or the poems of the Silesian Joseph von Eichendorff (a Prussian Ministerial Councillor). Distasteful? Strangely touching, if anything – this belated desire of an artificial state to give itself a soul for political reasons.

Prussia was not alone in this. In September 1815 the Tsar, the Emperor of Austria and the King of Prussia had concluded the 'Holy Alliance', a domestic and foreign-policy alliance against aggression and revolution, intended to make their three states 'members of one and the same Christian nation'. Here, too, we find Christianity as the political link – regardless of the fact that the Tsar was Orthodox, the Emperor of Austria Catholic and the King of Prussia Protestant. An undefined ecumenical universal Christianity served the 'Holy Alliance' as its ideology, just as it was intended to serve Frederick Wilhelm III's Prussia as a state ideology. There has been much scornful comment on this spiritual embroidery of the alliance between the Three Black Eagles', not only by opponents but also by participants; Metternich called it 'high-sounding nothingness'. But even Metternich took the alliance as such entirely seriously; it formed the power base of the European peace system which he had knocked together at the Congress of Vienna. The King of Prussia took it even more seriously. In his political testament of 1835 he enjoined his successor: 'Do not omit to promote concord among the European powers with all your strength. Above all, let Prussia, Russia and Austria never be separated from one another; their holding together should be seen as the keystone of the great European alliance.'

Compare this with the final sentences of Frederick the Great's political testament of 1776: 'So long as the country lacks greater cohesion and better frontiers its rulers must be *toujours en vedette*, keep an eye on their neighbours and be ready at any moment to ward off the ruinous conspiracies of their enemies.'

No greater contrast is conceivable. Prussia in 1835 lacked cohesive state territory and defendable frontiers as much as in 1776. Yet the conclusions which Frederick Wilhelm III drew from this situation were the exact opposite of those of his great predecessor. Frederick had concluded that Prussia must enlarge itself and had demanded of his state that 'everything about it should have strength, nerve and vitality'. Frederick Wilhelm concluded that Prussia must content itself and seek security in concord and unity with a 'great European alliance', in particular with Russia and Austria.

Frederick the Great had been lucky with his daring policy, but Frederick Wilhelm III was also lucky during the last twenty-five years of his reign: during those years of the restoration period and the 'Holy Alliance' there were no neighbours who were enemies or were hatching 'ruinous conspiracies'. Prussia was accepted; one might say: It had arrived. And it, in its turn, accepted the role assigned to it at the Congress of Vienna, even if it was not a grand role. Prussia now – for the first time in its history – was universally recognized as one of the five great powers with a say in Europe, albeit unmistakably in the fifth place. Within the narrower conservative alliance of the 'Three Black Eagles', which supported and guaranteed the new European order, it was an equal and enjoyed equal respect, though again clearly in the third place alongside the Russian and Austrian giants. And within the German Confederation, with which the Congress of Vienna had replaced the fallen Empire and in which Austria, in a matter-of-fact manner, occupied the place of the presiding power, Prussia, modestly and sensibly, contented itself with being permanently in second place. Throughout a lifetime, from 1815 to 1848, Prussia was a peaceful state within a peace system. The part it played within that peace system was not unlike that played by the Federal Republic of Germany within the European Community and NATO today.

Like the present-day European Community and North Atlantic Treaty Organization the European system created at the Congress of Vienna was a community of states amongst whom war was to be ruled out and in fact remained ruled out for a long time; it was a peace system. After the frightful upheavals and hardships of the preceding period of over twenty years of war peace had, for a whole generation, and for all European states, become the most precious thing, to which they readily subordinated their special interests. Austria no longer made a claim to Silesia, France reconciled itself to the loss of the Rhine frontier, and even Prussia no longer saw the raggedness of its ancient eastern and its new western territories as a justification for a 'rounding-up' policy. And, unlike the present-day European Community or NATO, the peace system of the Congress of Vienna embraced the whole of Europe. The victorious powers of 1813–15 had been wise enough to accept and fit vanquished France into the European system they had established, as a participant with equal rights and enjoying equal respect; they had preserved their wartime unity beyond the end of the war and indeed ideologically consolidated it, so that this peace did not divide Europe, as our present peace is doing, but united it. All that amounts to a remarkable statesmanlike achievement, unparalleled to this day, and one would do well to look at the advantages deriving from it and pay tribute to its exceptional character before considering the weaknesses from which ultimately – though only a generation later – it perished.

The weaknesses lay in a certain blindness towards ideas. The peace of 1815 was a peace between states. What the Congress of Vienna had striven for, and achieved, was the most perfect possible balance of power, one which, as Wilhelm von Humboldt said admiringly of the German Confederation, was to preserve itself 'by its immanent force of gravity'. State frontiers were so drawn and the spheres of influence of the great powers so balanced that a war to change them would not be worth anyone's while and would not promise anyone success. In fact, the peace system of 1815 was never upset by conflicts between states; what eventually unhinged it in 1848 was not a war but a revolution.

Yet that revolution had been threatening from the very beginning, and if King Frederick Wilhelm III referred to a 'great European alliance' whose 'keystone' was the alliance of the 'Three Black Eagles' – Russia, Austria, and Prussia – then this at first sight strange expression absolutely hit the mark. The European state system of 1815 was indeed an alliance – but not, as was customary, the alliance of one group of states against others, but the alliance of all states against a revolution by which all of them felt menaced: against the national, democratic and liberal forces awakened by the French Revolution and unleashed in the struggle against Napoleon. The nations had begun to be aware of their national identities and to demand democratic national states; a rising bourgeoisie desired liberal constitutions. The Congress of Vienna had disregarded these forces and desires – it had to disregard them if it was to achieve the perfect balance of power and, moreover, the solidarity of the states guaranteeing the peace. That peace between states had been bought – exaggerating a little – by a silent but continual war between the states and the peoples.

Not by any means, all peoples, and not the whole people. They, too, were weary of war and initially treasured the restored peace. Not for nothing is the period from 1815 to 1848 called the *Biedermeier* period, the age of the ordinary decent man. But beneath that idyllic surface things were in motion, and the subterranean thunder was growing louder all the time. At first it was only a student revolt, later a widespread bourgeois oppositional movement, and finally, in 1848, suddenly an all-European revolution. The national movements which were to break up the European Alliance system did not appear on the scene abruptly. First only the Italians and the Poles stirred; then the Belgians, the Hungarians and the Germans; and much later the Slav nations of the Austrian monarchy. Nevertheless, the history of this outwardly so uneventful restoration period is at the same time the history of a slowly gathering and silently ever more powerful national and liberal revolution which finally put an end to Restoration Europe.

Prussia's history during the epoch should be seen against that double background. One thing is immediately obvious: although Prussia quite deliberately and almost enthusiastically took its place in the 'grand European alliance' against revolution, unwittingly, and even against its will, it also had one foot in the other camp. The fact that in the Napoleonic era it had flirted with the ideas of the French Revolution could not be entirely forgotten or expunged; many of the Stein-Hardenberg reforms had still not been rescinded.

Besides, it still had – or rather again had – a strangely incomplete tattered territorial body. No one could quite forget that throughout its past history this very unsatisfactory territorial shape had driven Prussia towards a policy of expansion and aggrandisement. No matter how honestly it now foreswore such a policy, it was not entirely believed.

Finally, the national movement that was now slowly gathering momentum was not only a danger to Prussia but also an opportunity. For the Austrian multi-national state that national movement was pure dynamite. To Prussia it might become a temptation: Prussia was now, in spite of its Polish minority, no longer a two-nation state but a predominantly German state – the only almost purely German great power; and many German nationalists of the restoration period, for instance the Swabian Pfizer and the Hessian Gagern, had offered Prussia the leading role in Germany even before 1848. Officially Prussia, however, did not wish to consider such things then, and whenever the people uttering such ideas were Prussian subjects, like Arndt, Jahn or Schleiermacher, they were harassed and persecuted.

Prussia altogether played an inglorious part in the 'persecution of demagogues' during the twenties and thirties. The fact that many of the persecuted 'demagogues' – the liberal German nationalists who were dreaming of the future German bourgeois-national state – were pinning their best hopes on Prussia did not help them in the least with the Prussian authorities or with the Prussian courts of law. Prussia rejected any 'German mission' and even its own liberal past with that redoubled stubbornness that springs from an awareness of secret temptation; during the last twenty years of Frederick Wilhelm III's reign it acquired an unsavoury reputation as a police state favouring censorship. The strange thing was that, at the very same time, it was experiencing an entirely respectable flowering of its cultural life. While Heine and Görres were on the run from the Prussian censor – indeed from Prussian warrants for arrest – Schinkel and Rauch were beautifying Berlin and Mendelssohn discovered the St Matthew Passion. Academic life in *Biedermeier* Prussia also had a dual face. Never had the University of Berlin listed more brilliant names: Hegel and Schelling, Savigny and Ranke; yet at the same time hundreds of rebellious students disappeared behind prison walls. In the Berlin salons, which had first flourished in the Napoleonic era, there was still much wit about. A strange period of Prussian history, a kind of silver age: elegant stagnation, a stuffy idyll – and deepest peace; even the famous army had gone to sleep on its laurels. In 1864, after the storming of the Düppel Battlements, when a victory salute was to be fired on Unter den Linden, no one could be found who knew how many salvoes were the right number.

Not much happened during those 'quiet years', but quite a lot changed. The Prussia of 1815 had still been an almost exclusively agricultural state. During the next thirty years manufactures and industries developed; in the cities there was now a middle class which no longer lived off the court or the state, and at the same time a proletariat was coming into existence. The first railways began to operate in Prussia in the thirties. That, too, was the time of the customs agreements which opened a large part of Germany to the free movement of goods within the Prussian-German Customs Union. And along with the merchandise, ideas began to circulate – the new irreverent ideas of civil liberty and national unity. It was paradoxical: prior to 1813 Prussia's state-inspired will to reform had come up against a still intact agrarian-feudal social structure which had virtually paralysed it. After 1815 a new society developed, one positively crying out for reforms; but now it was the state that did not wish

to implement reforms and indeed quite stubbornly opposed any
innovation. The term 'stubborn' is particularly apt with regard
to the ageing King Frederick Wilhelm III. During the final decades
of his life he had become a person grown cautious and stoical by
the shocks he had experienced. He had always been peace-loving;
in his old age his need for peace and quiet acquired a grim trait,
one of hostility to life, something that shut windows and made
the air stuffy. The change of sovereign in 1840 had long been
hoped for; when it occurred, it did not change the policy but it
changed the atmosphere. Dismal winter turned into 'pre-March'.*

About the new King Frederick Wilhelm IV Heine – as we have
seen, no friend of Prussia – wrote the following lines of friendly
mockery:

> I have a weak spot for that King;
> I think we two are a little alike:
> A noble spirit, a lot of talent.
> I, too, would make a rotten ruler.

Not a bad characterization. A noble spirit with a lot of talent –
that Frederick Wilhelm IV really had, as well as a marked gift of
oratory of which he made ample use. His father had never made
a public speech, and even in private conversation had preferred
to utter nothing but infinitives and scraps of sentences ('Under-
standing it all – Fatal to me'). The son, immediately upon ascend-
ing the throne, surprised his subjects with a long sermon-like
speech, and soon made another at his Coronation, and again
subsequently on any occasion that offered itself. He desired to be
a monarch 'close to the people'; at the same time, even more so
than his sober father, he was permeated by a mystically romantic
concept of his Divine Right and with a downright revulsion against
modern constitutionalism, making the observation that throughout
Europe its soil had been 'manured with rivers of blood. In Germany it is only the alliance between Austria and Prussia that is
holding the wild beast, grinning, in its cage.'

If from such strong language one were to conclude that this

---

* The German word *Vormärz* describes the period from 1840 to the
revolution of March 1848.

was a hard despot one would be mistaken. Frederick Wilhelm IV was a soft, amiable character, and his favourite fighting stance was the embrace. He invariably wanted to disarm his enemies by humanity and obligingness, and in doing so frequently acted against his own convictions – and would then be profoundly disappointed and angered if he did not reap gratitude. His reign began with a general amnesty for the sentenced 'demagogues' and the rehabilitation of persecuted professors and journalists. This King of Prussia even received the radical revolutionary poet Georg Herwegh in audience and said to him: 'I love an opposition which shows character.' Herwegh was not won over.

It was the clash of this character with the revolution of 1848 that determined Prussia's history during the three tumultuous years 1848–50.

The revolution had been clearly seen to be approaching for at least two years, and Frederick Wilhelm, in his fashion, had tried at an early stage to take the wind out of its sails by meeting it halfway. In the spring of 1847 he used his sovereign royal power to summon a 'United Diet', a quasi-parliamentary assembly of all provincial 'estates', but instantly devalued that gesture in his opening address when he said that no power on earth would compel him to make it a permanent institution. His brother-in-law, the Tsar, remarked: 'A curious new regime: the King grants a constitution and denies that it is one.' The United Diet proved insubordinate and in the autumn was ungraciously dissolved. The demand for its 'periodicity' henceforward became a revolutionary slogan. The royal gesture had fizzled out. But the then most influential adviser to the King, Radowitz, already had a new idea: 'The King must win Prussia in and through Germany.'

That the King had always been ready to do. Even at the time of his accession to the throne he had proposed to Metternich 'action in concert with Austria's imperial power towards the elevation and glorification of our beloved German fatherland, in order thereby to achieve in the heart of Europe a dynamic unity and entity'. Metternich had always treated this with reserve and disinclination, and continued to do so. Very reluctantly Frederick Wilhelm was now persuaded by Radowitz to act without Austria:

a congress of German princes was to be convened in Potsdam with the intention of making the German Confederation into a federal state, with its own army, navy, customs union, federal court and freedom of the press – all this, it should be understood, as a gracious gift from above. As a very last concession, when revolution had broken out in France and Italy and the situation was getting increasingly alarming also in Vienna and Berlin, the King even granted what hurt him most: a federal parliament, composed of the 'estates' of the federal countries, and thus in God's name a permanent United Diet also in Prussia. On 18 March 1848 a Patent Royal announced the entire programme. Just then the battle of the barricades erupted in Berlin.

It is important to know this background in order to understand the King's attitude during the revolutionary days: the withdrawal of the troops from revolutionary Berlin, his ride through Berlin wearing a black-red-and-gold sash, his proclamation 'To my beloved Berliners', his famous dictum 'Prussia henceforward is absorbed into Germany'. It was not just that he had lost his nerve and could not bear to see blood. Of course it was frightful for him to hear his troops open fire on his 'beloved Berliners'. But, above all, everything seemed such a terrible misunderstanding: surely he had already freely and graciously granted everything, or nearly everything, that his subjects were now trying to extort from him by rebellion and violence!

He found himself swept away by the current, and what had been intended as a magnanimous royal gesture was now being implemented over his head. Throughout the summer Berlin was in the hands of a Citizens' Militia, a radical Prussian parliament was working on a radical Prussian constitution, in Frankfurt a German National Assembly was in session without having been called by the princes, and the King had to pocket humiliations. At the same time, however, the revolution ran out of steam during the summer of 1848. Basically, it had been more powerful while it was threatening than it was now that it had actually taken place. The fate of all revolutions is ultimately decided by who controls the armed forces. And the army, though withdrawn from Berlin by royal command in March, was still firmly in the hands of the King; in the autumn, upon royal command, it marched into Berlin again. It encountered no opposition. Parliament was adjourned and moved to Brandenburg on the Havel, then dissolved. The revolution in Prussia was over. The reins were once more firmly in the King's hands.

It is interesting that this did not immediately trigger off a period of reaction and repression. Frederick Wilhelm remained true to his character which was so strangely compounded of softness and stubbornness; he took no revenge but wished to be a magnanimous victor. Now that his hands were free again it seemed to him that the time had come to implement his March programme with a grand gesture: to grant, out of sovereign royal power, the Prussian constitution which the people had tried to extort from him, and then to unite Germany under Prussia's leadership – not through the people but, as was right and proper, through the princes.

Frederick Wilhelm and his advisers – who now once more all came from the state-supporting conservative aristocratic and civil service class – were confronted in the autumn of 1848 with the question: Must Prussia allow itself to be used by the German bourgeois revolution or might it use that revolution for its own ends? Did it have to become a bourgeois-parliamentarian state or could it, with a few constitutional concessions, preserve its character and restrain its bourgeoisie? Did it really have to 'be absorbed into Germany' or might it dominate Germany?

To start with, in 1849, Prussia decided all these questions in its own favour. By 1850 it already held, for a few months, a position of hegemony in Germany that was not very different from that held twenty years later. But what was achieved twenty years later was not what resulted at this first attempt. Prussia's German policy in 1849–50 succeeded in checking the German revolution, in dominating it and in turning it to Prussia's advantage. What it failed to accomplish was its breakaway from the alliance of the 'three Black Eagles'. Prussia in 1850 failed not because of Germany but because of its old partners, rivals and opponents: Austria and Russia.

In the first place, on 5 December 1848, the King gave Prussia a constitution by Royal Patent. This 'imposed' constitution, which with only slight amendments remained in force until 1918, in its contents entirely harmonized with the liberal demands of the day. It guaranteed all the essential basic rights, an independent judiciary, freedom for the press and freedom of assembly, and a freely elected parliament, initially even on a 'one man one vote' basis. The Prussian three-class suffrage, which subsequently became so notorious, was introduced as an amendment by parliament itself a few years later. It was nothing unusual in the eyes of the time. In Britain and France, and in other countries with parliamentary constitutions, it was then also regarded as a matter of course that the vote was tied to certain property and income qualifications, to a 'census'. And the Prussian Chambers based on a class vote were by no means willing yes-men parliaments: in the sixties they regularly produced liberal majorities and during the famous constitutional conflict, which will be mentioned in the next chapter, they brought a Prussian King to the brink of abdication.

But all that was still in the future. For the moment the revolution was over in Prussia and domestic peace had been restored by the 'imposed' constitution. Prussia could now turn to Germany and to the programme for German unification which the King had proclaimed on 18 March, a few hours before the outbreak of the revolution in Berlin. That programme had envisaged a German federal state by agreement with the ruling princes – certainly not a people's state; to Frederick Wilhelm IV a vital difference.

Bearing in mind his views it was inevitable that he should decline the German imperial crown offered to him by the Frankfurt National Assembly in April 1849. To accept it would have meant placing himself at the head of the German revolution – moreover, when he had only just crushed the revolution in Prussia. Nothing could be further from his mind. But German unity, and under Prussian leadership – that he wanted too; except that this was to be an anti-revolutionary and not a revolutionary unity. In the spring of 1848 his plan had been for a federation of princes to anticipate the German revolution; a year later such a federation was to put an end to the revolution just as the imposed constitution had put an end to it in Prussia.

The final fling of the revolution, which took place in Saxony, Baden and the Palatinate in May 1849, following the dissolution of the Frankfurt National Assembly, provided the opportunity: the rebellion was crushed by the Prussian army at the request of the hard-pressed regional princes – often, especially in Baden, with shocking brutality; the Prussian courts-martial have not been forgotten in Rastatt in Baden to this day. Be that as it may, Prussian troops were now stationed in Saxony, in Hesse, and in Baden; and Prussia appeared to be in a position, as the victor, to impose upon Germany the unity which the revolution had been unable to give it. In the summer of 1849 the Prussian King established the 'German Union', a league of twenty-eight German princes who were forced to participate whether they liked it or not. Fear of revolution was still very much in their bones, and Prussia, which had coped with its own revolution, seemed to be the only, or at any rate the safest, bulwark against revolution and therefore could dictate its conditions: a federal state, a federal army and a federal constitution. True, Bavaria and Württemberg opted out; these two sovereign German kingdoms felt strong enough on their own and were, moreover, particularly disinclined to enter into close ties with that total stranger Prussia. Otherwise, however, the German Union of 1850 already foreshadowed the full scope of the later German empire of 1871. Once again Prussia had been successful with its ancient methods – surprise, rapid action, lightning-like change of position and, at the decisive moment, once again the sharp sword. Its leading position in Germany seemed secure.

Even the bourgeois liberals joined in. A rump of the dissolved Frankfurt National Assembly, convened in Gotha, gave the Prussian-German Union its democratic blessings: 'The objectives which were to have been achieved by the [Frankfurt] Reich constitution are more important than any rigid clinging to the form by which these objectives were to have been attained.' One year after the dissolution of the Assembly in Frankfurt a German constitution was once more worked out, in Erfurt – this time under Prussian patronage.

And then, suddenly, everything collapsed, as though it had never happened: a collapse as complete as that of 1806. The Jena of 1850 was Olmütz. As on that earlier occasion, Prussia again failed in the face of superior foreign power. Except that this time it did not even risk a hopeless war but surrendered from the outset.

The reason why in 1849 Prussia had been able to act with such sovereignty in Germany was not only the weakness of its German opponents and partners; the bourgeoisie's fear of power, the short-windedness of the proletarian rebels on the barricades, or the intimidation of the princes. It was mainly to be found in the fact that the traditional German leading power, Austria, was still paralysed by its own revolution, not the bourgeois-proletarian revolution in Vienna which Austria had crushed in November 1848 just as decisively as Prussia had overcome its own in Berlin, but the national revolution of its alien component nations. Throughout 1849 Austria still had to wage war in Italy and Hungary: in Hungary it was eventually victorious only thanks to Russian help. During that time it could not concern itself with Germany. But by 1850 it was once more able to do so. Austria returned like a wrathful Ulysses; found its German mansion occupied by the Prussians and decided to have a ruthless clean-up.

In this enterprise Austrian policy displayed an untypical, energetic, overbearing, indeed insolent trait which bore the handwriting of its new 'strong man', Schwarzenberg – a man who might have turned all German history into a totally different direction if he had not suddenly died in 1852. Schwarzenberg had his own grand overall concept for Germany: he wanted not only to restore the German Confederation but to bring the whole of the Habsburg monarchy into it, including its Hungarian, Italian and southern Slav parts, which meant in effect attaching Germany to Austria – to the ancient great Austria. His vision was not a national Germany but a supra-national central Europe, a genuine 'empire' with its centre in Vienna : the vision of Charles V and Wallenstein. For Prussia, as it had developed over the past century, there was scarcely room in this concept: that ambitious semi-great power would only have been a disturbing factor. Asked what he intended to do with Prussia in his Greater Germany, Schwarzenberg is said to have replied '*Avilir, puis démolir*' – weaken it, then demolish it. For the moment he treated anything that Prussia had done in Germany during 1848–50 as if it did not exist; he reconvened the old Frankfurt Assembly as if nothing had happened; he persuaded Saxony and Hanover to defect from the Union; and he finally gave Prussia an ultimatum to pull out from Hesse. In the autumn Prussia and Austria were mobilizing against each other. War seemed inevitable.

At that moment the Tsar intervened, and he did so on the side of Austria. True, he did not share Schwarzenberg's long-term goal – indeed the idea of a German-Austrian giant empire at the gates of Russia must have seemed to him rather alarming – nor was he interested in a weakened, let alone a demolished, Prussia. He simply wanted the *status quo* – neither Schwarzenberg's great empire in central Europe nor Prussia's German Union but quite simply the *status quo ante* 1848, the old alliance of the 'three Black Eagles' against nationalism and revolution. This, however, for the moment, made him an ally of Austria since Schwarzenberg's central European empire was still a mere plan whereas Prussia's German Union was very nearly a reality. That reality had to be swept away first of all. Prussia must not be allowed to benefit from its opportunist playing with revolution; everything had to be once more as it had been prior to 1848. That was his demand now – and under the combined pressure of Austria and Russia, its ancient protectors and allies who were now suddenly showing such angry faces, Prussia surrendered at Olmütz on 29 November 1850 – unconditionally and totally. The Union was dissolved, the old German Confederation of 1815 was revived unchanged, anything that Prussia had done in Germany was undone. The disgrace was undisguised and unmitigated. Prussia came out of Olmütz like a whipped schoolboy who had been caught out in a naughty prank and now promised with deep blushes that he would never do it again. It was a defeat like that of 1806, except that this time no blood was shed.

The curious thing was that, once again, Prussia accepted its defeat with a certain stoicism, that it adjusted itself and tried to make the best of it; this time, in fact, with more goodwill and conviction than on the earlier occasion. Then adaptation had meant reforms – a liberalizing reconstruction of the state, vigorously opposed by the nucleus of Prussian society, the state-supporting military aristocracy. Now adaptation meant conservative restoration and reaction, something that suited that class perfectly. Many Prussian conservatives had been far from easy about Frederick Wilhelm's high-flying German experiments from the start and, as far as their reaction to Olmütz was concerned, pain at the humiliation was outweighed by the grim satisfaction that they had always been saying so and had now been proved right. Unlike their sentimental King they had never 'been pierced by a shudder of enthusiasm at the word Germany'. The Deputy Bismarck, for instance, had dryly observed at the Erfurt Union Parliament: 'We want a federal state, but if this constitution were to be its price we would rather do without it.' Six months later, in the Berlin Parliament, he defended Olmütz: 'It is not Prussia's task to act the Don Quixote everywhere in Germany.' The alliance with the 'German-national swindle' had been profoundly distasteful to him, as it had been to most Prussian conservatives. The ancient well-tested alliance of the 'three Black Eagles' was something far more solid, and the Prussian conservatives were happy to see it now restored – or seemingly restored. During the next few years after Olmütz Prussia again devoted itself to the re-establishment of that alliance with sentimental enthusiasm – the enthusiasm of the prodigal son returned home.

Except that none of this was any use. The alliance was not to be re-established in the long run, its time had run out and it broke up. This was no fault of Prussia's – any more than the alliance between Napoleon and Alexander had broken up through Prussia's fault forty years earlier. It was the Crimean War which turned Austria and Russia from friends into enemies between 1854 and 1856 – moreover, as it turned out, for ever. In that war between the Western powers and Russia the issue, for the first time, was the Turkish succession in the Balkans, a hotbed of crisis which would not let European politics come to rest for over half a century and would eventually become the flashpoint of the First World War. Prussia and Austria both remained neutral in the Crimean War, but their neutrality was of a very different character: Prussia, in a manner of speaking, was neutral on the Russian side while Austria was neutral on the Western side. Austria had intended to exploit the Crimean War for acquiring the Danubian principalities (present-day southern and eastern Romania) and squeezing Russia out of the Balkans; all this regardless of the fact that a mere five years earlier Russia had saved Austria from defeat in the Hugarian revolutionary war. 'Austria will amaze the world yet by its ingratitude,' Schwarzenberg had declared on that earlier occasion; a typical remark. Austria and Russia became mortal rivals in the Balkans, and Prussia could no longer be the third man in the alliance quite simply because the alliance no longer existed. Prussia now had to choose between them, whether it wished to or not.

It was not only the alliance of the 'three Black Eagles' which had come to an end: the entire exquisite European system established by Metternich in 1815, the system in which Prussia had so willingly come to rest, had broken up through the revolutions and their consequences. France was no longer playing. Another Napoleon was now on the throne, and even though that 'third' Napoleon lacked the imperial ambitions of the first, he certainly had the ambition to shift the centre of European politics from Vienna to Paris. His instrument was an alliance with nationalism: at first Italian nationalism, with which he was successful; then Polish nationalism, with no result; and finally even German nationalism, which broke his neck. At any rate, he made sure of unrest in Europe, of war and of rumours of war. Post-revolutionary Europe was no longer that peaceful community of states it had been from 1815 to 1848. Each state was on its own again; including, whether it liked it or not, Prussia.

German pre-revolutionary conditions could no more be restored than those of Europe, even though the German Confederation was again meeting in Frankfurt as if nothing had ever happened. Neither the national nor the bourgeois-liberal movements had lost their dynamism through the defeat of 1849–49. The German bourgeois national movement remained in a state of permanent turbulence, a factor to be taken into account and to be tackled in one way or another. Besides, with the now rapid progress of industrialization the bourgeoisie was growing increasingly powerful during the fifties and sixties, and in the early sixties that industrialization also produced the beginnings of an organized working-class movement – with its centre in Prussia. By 1860, in a different way, the situation was once more very much as it had been ten years earlier: revolution as such might have been shelved but the German bourgeoisie with its National Association and Progressive Party was once more massively gaining ground, and Austria and Prussia were engaged in an inescapable rivalry for its favour; both were passing through a seemingly irresistible domestic liberalization and 'parliamentarization' process, both were anxious to make 'moral conquests' in Germany, both were eager to channel the flow of the national movement through their own millraces, both were competing with reform plans for the German Confederation. Prussia had the advantage of being unencumbered by Austria's tricky nationality problems; Austria had the advantage of being greater and stronger and probably also more popular, and mainly of still being the traditional leading power in Germany, the ancient imperial power.

The eventual outcome of all that was still entirely open in the early sixties. Numerous solutions were in the air: a closer and a looser federation, a German dualism with Prussian predominance in northern and Austrian in southern Germany, a reform of the existing German Confederation in the direction of parliamentarianism. One thing was expected by everybody: a substantial increase in the power of the bourgeois-parliamentary institutions throughout Germany. One thing was not expected by anyone: a war between the two German powers.

That both expectations were disappointed, that Prussia became an imperial power and Austria a foreign country – that was the work of a single man who was still a political outsider in his own state in the early sixties: Bismarck.

6

PRUSSIA'S FOUNDATION OF THE
GERMAN EMPIRE

*'King Bismarck the First' – Politics Dictated by the Need for
Success – 1866: Prussia's Goal Achieved – 1870: An Accident
and an Improvisation*

BISMARCK CONTINUES to live in the German mind as the
founder of the German Empire, and there has been an enormous
amount of discussion – and no doubt there will be more in the
future – about whether his foundation of the Empire was a blessing or a disaster for Germany. On the other hand, astonishingly
little thought has been given to the question of whether the
foundation of the German Empire was a blessing or a disaster
for Prussia; and this is the more surprising since Bismarck himself undoubtedly looked upon it primarily from the Prussian
point of view and accomplished it as an action of Prussian policy.

Bismarck was not a German nationalist; he was a Prussian
statesman. Not only in his early political period but also during
his time as Prussian Minister President, the term 'German-
national swindle' readily dropped from his lips, and in 1866 he
had not the least national scruples about waging war against the
greater part of non-Prussian Germany as well as against Austria;
in one of the many nerve-racking arguments with King Wilhelm I
which preceded that war, the King once exclaimed in exaspera-
tion: 'But are you not a German as well?' On the other hand,
whenever he refers to Prussia, a real warmth rings through
Bismarck's words: 'God will know how long Prussia shall exist'
he wrote in a private letter. 'But God knows I shall be very sorry
when it ceases!'

And yet, more than any other single person, Bismarck contributed to it that Prussia 'ceased' – not through political failure or mismanagement, but, paradoxically, through too much success. He raised Prussia to heights where it could not breathe in the long run. By founding the Empire, which made Prussia the predominant power in Germany and Germany the predominant power in Europe, he may have overstretched Germany – that is something one may argue about – but undoubtedly he injected Prussia with the germ of its own destruction: alongside and within a united Germany Prussia was bound progressively to lose its independence, its identity and eventually its existence. It became superfluous, an anomaly within the structure of the German Reich; and in the end it became the victim of a failed German world policy – a policy which Prussia as Prussia could have never pursued or indeed envisaged.

The historian Walter Bussmann observes:

When Bismarck allied himself to the national idea, one of the driving forces of the century, he wanted to benefit the Prussian state, but in an objective sense he simultaneously served the cause of a national state, the objective of his political opponents.

One might put it even more pointedly: the alliance between the Prussian idea of the state and the German national idea was an alliance between fire and water; and though it may seem at times as if a strong fire might turn water to steam, in the end the fire will be extinguished by the water. Bismarck's foundation of the Empire appeared to his contemporaries as Prussia's greatest triumph; in the final analysis it proved to be the beginning of Prussia's decline. Even so, the end did not expunge the triumph. Few states have gone to their ruin more gloriously than Bismarck's Prussia.

Bismarck's Prussia – we use or read that phrase as if it were a matter of course, but we should do well to stop for a moment, consider the phrase and wonder at it. It is a fact: from the moment he became Prussian Minister President, Bismarck sovereignly shaped Prussian politics – and what politics! – but how was that possible? Surely Bismarck was not a Prussian sovereign. Political decisions in Prussia had always been made by the King: Frederick Wilhelm I and Frederick the Great had made them personally; their successors consulted Ministers and advisers; but that a mere Minister should determine Prussian policy for a number of years and decades, just as though he were the King – as early as 1865 the British Foreign Minister Clarendon mockingly referred to 'King Bismarck the First' – was unheard of in Prussia, even in the heyday of Hardenberg, between 1810 and 1815, when a deeply discouraged and humiliated king, by nature irresolute, had given his Chancellor more than the customary freedom of action.

Yet Wilhelm I, Bismarck's lifelong King, was a much stronger ruler by nature than Frederick Wilhelm III. Admittedly, the title 'the Great', which his grandson posthumously tried to award him, has never stuck to his name. But among the kings of Prussia he undoubtedly belongs in the top rank. One might call him Prussia's second soldier king: he was a soldier to the core, an experienced professional officer; the Prussian army reform is due to him, and without it Bismarck's wars would have taken a far less smooth and favourable course. Similarly the appointment of the inconspicuous but outstandingly efficient Chief of Staff Moltke can be personally credited to the King, and finally the subordination of operational command to the General Staff, an exclusively Prussian prescription for success, was introduced by Wilhelm I and practised for a long time ahead. Alongside his certainly above-average military competence Wilhelm I possessed solid sound common sense, a lot of political experience – he was sixty-four when he became King – and a strong monarchic pride. He was anything but a shadow King, and no one would have predicted that throughout his long reign – unexpectedly long as he did not die until 1888 at the age of ninety-one – he would stand in the shadow of his formidable Minister President and subsequent Reich Chancellor. Nor was there ever any natural affinity or human bond between Wilhelm I and Bismarck. Quite a short time before he made Bismarck his First Minister, in an hour of extreme predicament, the King had remarked that the man made him uneasy and inspired in him some inner distaste; and Bismarck, for his part, never ceased to complain of the expenditure of nervous energy which the eternal struggle with the King, and for the King's acquiescence, demanded of him.

This continuous struggle should not be lost sight of whenever one considers Bismarck's achievement. It, more than anything else, explains an important feature of Bismarck's policy especially during the first, the most eventful and dramatic, eight years, the years of the foundation of the Empire, the German Reich. Reference has often been made to Bismarck's 'Bonapartism', and a Napoleonic trait has been discovered in his policies between 1862 and 1871. In one respect that is incorrect: Bismarck was no usurper and would never have dreamed of putting himself in the place of the legitimate king; 'Revolution in Prussia is only made by the kings,' he said on one occasion. But one thing Bismarck really did have in common with the Bonapartes: like them he was under permanent pressure to produce successes – not, like them, to maintain an illegitimate throne but simply in order to maintain his position. After all, the King could dismiss him at any time – as Wilhelm II actually did much later – and there certainly was no shortage of enemies working for his overthrow (even in the King's closest entourage) nor of rivals who believed they could do better and would have liked to replace him. He was compelled to make himself indispensable at all times; for that he needed continuous crises (because one does not change horses in mid-stream) and continuous successes (because a successful Minister is not so easily dismissed). This explains, on the one hand, the pugnacity with which Bismarck, during his first years of government, positively sought out and exacerbated crises, and, on the other, the 'watchmaker's care' (a happy phrase coined by Bismarck's biographer Ludwig Reiners) which he applied, time and again, to their solution. It also explains something more important: the success fixation which compelled Bismarck not only to despise principles and not to be over-fastidious in the choice of his means, but even to change his objectives according to which seemed to promise the quickest and surest results.

Bismarck himself, in his old age, when he was working on his myth, occasionally described matters as though he had aimed at the foundation of the Empire from the very beginning, with the triumphal scene of the proclamation of the Emperor at the Palace of Versailles always – through all his moves and detours – invariably before his inner eye as the unassailable ultimate goal. Nothing could be more wrong. 'Monotony in action was never for me,' he said himself. What goals he laid down for Prussian politics at one time or another always depended upon what happened to be most promising. With regard to the Danish war of 1864, for instance, he once quite disarmingly let the cat out of the bag in a speech:

> I have always held to the priority scale whereby Personal Union [between Denmark and Schleswig-Holstein] was better than what existed at the time, that an independent ruler was better than Personal Union, and that unification with the Prussian State was better than an independent ruler. Which of these was attainable – that only events could show.

It was the same in the war with Austria and Germany in 1866 and in the war with France in 1870: the objectives each time depended on their attainability, and not on their desirability. One might almost call this the secret of Bismarck's successes: the man who always chooses an attainable goal can be reasonably sure of always attaining it. There is, of course, the danger that what has been attained may ultimately prove not worth the effort. As for the foundation of the German Reich, there are sufficient indications to show that Bismarck himself for a long time was in doubt about whether this was desirable for Prussia; and of more interest than the feat itself are the measures which Bismarck took against the risks which it held for Prussia and of which he was certainly aware. But the time has come to give a brief outline of the history of Prussia's foundation of the German Reich by Bismarck – Prussia's history during the highly dramatic years between 1862 and 1871.

Bismarck owed his appointment to the post of Prussian Minister President in September 1862 to a grave constitutional conflict which had broken out between King and Parliament about the army reform referred to above, set in motion by the King himself. It was a situation of the kind that, two centuries earlier, had triggered off the great Civil War in England and had eventually cost King Charles I his head: King and Parliament were in conflict about supreme control of the armed forces. Neither side wanted to give in. Wilhelm I, left in the lurch by his Ministers, terrified by his family with horror stories of the decapitation of Charles I of England, was about to abdicate when Bismarck, who had made a reputation for himself as a ruthless monarchist reactionary, offered himself as a last resort.

The temptation to speculate on the future course of Prussian history if Wilhelm I had in fact abdicated, as he intended, in 1862 is quite irresistible. His son Frederick III would not, in that case, have reigned for a mere three months – as he was to do – but for twenty-six years. Frederick III was a liberal. Under the influence of his politically very active English wife he would have put an end to the constitutional conflict by giving in and would have transformed the Prussian monarchy into a parliamentary monarchy on the English model. Prussia would have become a small continental Britain. Under the royal couple Frederick and Victoria no one would ever have heard of Bismarck. It seems most improbable that a Prussia with a parliamentary government could ever have united Germany against the opposition of France, Russia, Austria and the medium-sized German states solely with the help of the German liberals and the sympathies of Britain. But it seems entirely conceivable that, in such a case, Prussia might still exist today.

That was a mere diversion – let us now return to reality. Bismarck commended himself to the King as his loyal squire who would uphold royal rule against parliamentary government all the way to the execution block. Thereby he made himself indispensable to the King for the time being. But he staged no *coup d'état*. Instead he cleverly kept the constitutional conflict unresolved for the next five years, until eventually, in a totally changed situation, it was settled by parliament yielding in substance and the King yielding in form. Those five years Bismarck used for a series of bold, daring and exceedingly unpopular foreign-policy operations, alarming even to the King, but precisely calculated and crowned with brilliant success, though associated with two brief wars – the final result being an entirely new Prussia and an entirely new Germany.

Bismarck, by his entire background, was a strict conservative, an adherent of Metternich's system and a fierce opponent of liberalism, nationalism and the 1848 revolution. In 1850, as we have seen, he had defended the Olmütz surrender and, for this very reason, was soon afterwards sent as Prussian emissary to the Assembly in Frankfurt, where he remained for eight years. But in those eight years he learnt to change his views.

The fact was that Bismarck was not only a conservative, but was also a dyed-in-the-wool Prussian, and he was a realist. As a Prussian he was affronted by the overbearing Austrian policy of the Schwarzenberg era with which he found himself confronted in Frankfurt. As a realist he saw that the break between Austria and Russia since the Crimean War was irremediable and that the old European system was being increasingly shaken by Napoleon III's revisionist policy. As early as 1856 he concluded 'that in the not too distant future we shall have to fight against Austria for our existence' and that it should be possible to gain Russia's and France's benevolent neutrality in that event. Indeed, he went even further. Prussia's struggle against Austria would necessarily unroll in and for Germany – 'After Vienna's policy Germany is too narrow for both of us: we both plough the same contentious field' – and in Germany, too, Prussia needed allies. Being the realist he was, Bismarck knew that the German princes could never be such allies. In 1859 he told a startled interviewer that Prussia had but one real ally in Germany: the German people. The realist in Bismarck was stronger than the conservative. As a realist he was ready to make a pact with nationalism and indeed even with democracy.

Those were the foreign policy ideas and plans with which Bismarck in 1862 assumed his post in Prussia, and five years later they were all accomplished – admittedly by strange roundabout methods.

Bismarck's first foreign-policy action was an act of sabotage. In 1863 he caused the failure of Austria's attempt to breathe fresh life into the German Confederation – which in Bismarck's mind had already been sentenced to death – by means of a reform. An assembly of German princes was summoned to Frankfurt by Austria for this task, and indeed it was held with much pomp – but without Prussia. Bismarck persuaded his king after terrible arguments to stay away from it, and since the assembly of princes could not achieve anything without Prussia it dispersed without having accomplished anything. Thus the Austrian–Prussian conflict over the German issue had been publicly proclaimed for the first time. On this issue the two powers were now declared opponents.

Nevertheless – or just because of that – they became allies in 1864 in a war against Denmark, which was about Schleswig-Holstein. Annexation of the then Danish Schleswig-Holstein to Germany was one of the principal demands of German nationalism, and just because they were rivals for Germany neither Austria nor Prussia could avoid adopting this cause the moment it became topical again. Armed clashes about Schleswig-Holstein had first occurred in 1848. A congress of powers in London had then decided that Schleswig-Holstein should remain united with Denmark but only in Personal Union. Now the Danish King had died without issue and divergent successions in Denmark and Schleswig-Holstein had made Personal Union impossible; Denmark, therefore, setting aside the London protocol, annexed Schleswig. As co-signatories of the London protocol Austria and Prussia thereupon faced Denmark with an ultimatum to reverse the annexation. The war began on 1 February 1864.

With the assault on the Düppel battlements the war provided the Prussian Army with its first opportunity for demonstrating the quality it had regained through King Wilhelm's army reform – but that was the least of it. In military terms there was not much glory to be won in a war fought by two great powers against little Denmark. The difficult thing was to prevent the intervention of the other great powers which, after all, were all signatories to the London protocol, and among whom Britain in particular sided with Denmark. Intervention was in effect avoided, partly thanks to Bismarck's shrewd moderation – much to the outrage of German public opinion he did not demand a closer association of

Schleswig-Holstein with Germany but only the strict restoration of the *status quo* – and thanks partly to the obduracy with which Denmark clung to its annexation of Schleswig in contravention of the protocol. The outcome, at any rate, was that Denmark was compelled, with the tacit agreement of all powers, to hand over Schleswig-Holstein to Austria and Prussia, to be jointly disposed of by them as they saw fit. This was of no particular use to Austria – what was it to do with far-distant Schleswig-Holstein? – but for Prussia it was not only a chance of territorial gain but, above all, it represented an apple of discord over which Bismarck, and this was his main interest, might at any time trigger off a war between Prussia and Austria.

Not that he positively wanted such a war. 'Many roads were leading to my goal,' he said later. 'I had to choose one after another in turn, the most dangerous of them last.' What he was aiming at was the dissolution of the German Confederation, which he felt to be an irritating shackle on Prussian policy, and Prussia's unrestricted hegemony in northern Germany. Southern Germany he was prepared to cede to an analagous Austrian hegemony. If this objective could be achieved by peaceful agreement with Austria, so much the better.

It is true that even such a peaceful agreement on the partition of Germany along the Main line was not to be obtained without pressure, and throughout the two years between the Danish and the German wars Bismarck was ceaselessly working towards Austria's international isolation. In Russia, which was Austria's permanent rival in the Balkans anyway, this was easy. In France it was more difficult because the France of Napoleon III had its own plans. It was hoping to be the profiteering party in a war between Austria and Prussia, and to gain, as the price of arbitration in favour of the loser, certain 'compensations' on the left bank of the Rhine, perhaps even the Rhine as a frontier. This Bismarck could not and would not concede if he did not wish to risk a break with his other ally, German nationalism; but he was entirely willing to give vague and non-committal assurances to the Emperor Napoleon. Napoleon, incidentally, expected Prussia to be the loser in an Austrian–Prussian war, and he was prepared to save its life for a substantial mediation fee – not an unreasonable expectation in view of the difference in size of the two contestants. Bismarck, too, realized that a war against Austria could easily be lost – indeed, on form, was bound to be lost. Austria was still the bigger and stronger of the two. That, just as much as his fundamental disinclination to wage war (based mainly on the reflection that in a war policies are always in danger of being steam-rollered by military considerations) made him hesitate. Although Bismarck never shrank from war as the ultimate tool of policy, he always tried to avoid it if possible. This was true of the war of 1866 and, even more so, as we shall see, of that of 1870.

In contrast to 1870, he at least in 1866 had objectives which were unattainable without the risk of war or the threat of war, and this threat of war behind them deprived the peace proposals he made to Austria of their credibility. Three times there were held between Prussia and Austria what might be termed pre-war peace negotiations: at Schönbrunn in 1864, in Gastein in 1865, and again, shortly before the outbreak of war, by the 'Gablenz Mission' in Vienna in 1866. Only in Gastein was something like a partial result achieved, the partition of Schleswig-Holstein: Schleswig came under Prussian and Holstein under Austrian administration. But both sides realized that this was, at best, an armistice and not peace. What was really at stake was not the partition of Schleswig-Holstein but the partition of Germany between Austria and Prussia. And for that Austria was the less prepared, as Bismarck, in his struggle for Germany, was continually making deals with nationalism and democracy – deals which Austria, because of the nature of its empire, could not emulate. Even in his negotiations with Austria Bismarck demanded a German parliament elected by equal suffrage, though with limited competence. On all major questions of foreign and military policy Austria was to remain the decisive power in the south and Prussia in the north. But the kind of freely elected all-German parliament that Bismarck demanded would have represented a revolution even if its powers were restricted and even if the Austrian Germans had been able to vote for it – and to participate in a virtual revolution, especially under threat of war, was unacceptable to Austria. In the end it was Austria which first lost patience and mobilized. The 'war guilt question' of 1866 must therefore remain open. Only two points are certain: in the great political controversies which eventually led to the war Prussia had been the aggressor while Austria had been the defender of the *status quo*. And in the war itself Prussia was victorious – a surprise victor.

'The heavens are falling!' the Papal Cardinal State Secretary exclaimed when he read the news that Prussia had decisively defeated the united Austrians and Saxons at Königgrätz on 3 July 1866, the greatest battle of the century. But what was more serious, the heavens were falling at Königgrätz also upon the Emperor Napoleon. His whole policy had been based upon the probability of a Prussian defeat: he would then have saved Prussia from ruin and collected his price for doing so. He, and the whole of political France with him, now felt somehow cheated by the Prussian victory, and that explains the strange slogan of 'Revenge for Sadowa' ('Sadowa' was the French name for the battle of Königgrätz), a slogan that became powerful in French politics after 1866. Certainly the Franco-Prussian entente of the years leading up to 1866 – always an entente with ulterior motives on both sides – was finished at a stroke. Napoleon stayed the arm of the German victor.

He publicly proclaimed his armed peace mediation and despatched his emissary to Prussian headquarters. This made the situation of the victor of Königgrätz suddenly exceedingly precarious: if he rejected French mediation he would run the risk of a war on two fronts, a war without an end in sight; if he accepted it it would cost him territorial concessions on the Rhine – and the support of the German nationalists. The only way out was a rapid peace with Austria.

That was the course chosen by Bismarck, and the result, as far as Austria was concerned, was the most generous peace that had probably ever been concluded between victor and vanquished: no territorial concessions, no war reparations, immediate return of prisoners, immediate withdrawal from all occupied territories. Gaining acceptance for that peace cost Bismarck a terrific argument with his King, bringing Bismarck close to a nervous break-down and, according to his own assertion, to the verge of suicide. He did not succeed in convincing the King of the need for 'such an ignominious peace'. But he did prevail in the end. That crisis, which occurred at the Moravian castle of Nikolsburg during the final days of July 1866, remained the finest hour of his entire astonishing career.

Scarcely less generous were the peace treaties with the southern German states which had all fought against Prussia by the side of Austria and had lost the war: they too (with an insignificant exception in Hesse-Darmstadt) did not have to surrender any territory or pay reparations; they too remained unoccupied. All that was demanded of them was a military alliance with Prussia – to which they agreed with a sense of relief. Besides, for the first and only time in their history they now became internationally independent, completely sovereign states. They no longer, as had been the case until 1806, had a German Empire over them as a common protection, nor, as after 1815, a German Confederation. They were expressly permitted to associate in a new 'South German Confederation' if they so desired, but they never took that up. The fact that there was no longer any question of Austrian hegemony in southern Germany suited them very well.

Bismarck now proceeded in northern Germany all the more radically. After all, to expand Prussia in northern Germany had been Bismarck's real war aim, and this he now accomplished by means of radical annexations. Schleswig-Holstein, Hanover, Kurhessen and Hesse-Nassau all became Prussian provinces; even the hitherto Free City of Frankfurt – incidentally the only occupied territory that had been brutally treated in the war (such a huge contribution was extorted from it under threat of pillage that the Mayor committed suicide) – was annexed to Prussia. Prussia now achieved its greatest and final expansion, in a history so rich in conquest and territorial acquisitions. Within its frontiers it comprised nearly the whole of northern Germany, and by and large it has to be admitted that it successfully digested these huge annexations. Its ancient territorial elasticity and its talent for making Prussian rule acceptable to 'compulsory Prussians' through efficient administration, strict observance of the law and detached toleration once more proved itself – for the last time. Only in Hanover did a Guelph opposition hold out for a few more decades.

Perhaps it would have been in line with Prussia's style to make a proper job of it and incorporate also whatever north German territories and mini-territories remained; but surely it could not very well annex its own allies – Mecklenburg, Oldenburg, the Hanseatic cities and the majority of the small Thuringian principalities. As for Saxony, which had been high on Bismarck's annexation list, Austria had demanded considerate treatment in the peace treaty: the Saxons had fought bravely on Austria's side at Königgrätz and suffered heavy losses. Perhaps it would have been wiser if Prussia had left Saxony and the small north German principalities alone, or if it had merely demanded from them treaties of alliance as it had done in southern Germany. They certainly could never represent a danger to the great Prussia of 1866; many of them were now mere enclaves within Prussian territory. But Bismarck had concluded an alliance with German nationalism too. He had to have something to show to the German nationalists, something that they could view at least as a first instalment towards the unification of Germany. He had, moreover, promised them a freely elected German parliament – a German, not a Prussian, one. To democratize Prussia was the last thing he was prepared to do. So he conceived a way out. He invented the North German Confederation.

The North German Confederation was a strange contraption. Prussia itself, following the annexations of 1866, had twenty-four million inhabitants; the remaining twenty-two members of the North German Confederation together had six million. A Prussian Liberal referred to the 'coexistence of a dog with its fleas'. Nevertheless, the twenty-two little ones were nominally equal to the big one; to that extent the North German Confederation was a league of states. It was given a 'Reichstag', a parliament freely elected throughout the federation's territory by universal and equal suffrage, and equipped with extensive legislative and budgetary powers; to that extent it was a federal state. It was also to provide the framework into which, if the course of events led to that contingency, the southern German states could be fitted one day. Prussia itself, on the other hand, was to remain what it was, without any change. It was a squaring of the circle.

Bismarck himself seems to have realized that he was under-taking something contradictory. 'Formally one will have to incline towards a confederation of states, but in practice give it the character of a federal state by means of elastic, insignificant-sounding but far-reaching expressions,' he said in his instructions for the drafting of the North German Confederation's constitution. How that was to be done was not stated. One has the impression that Bismarck himself was not for once entirely clear about what precisely he wanted. He tolerated – much against his usual habit – amendments to his constitutional draft on no fewer than forty points by the North German Reichstag elected in the autumn of 1866, including one on the most important point. In Bismarck's draft the 'Federal Chancellor' was to have been no more than Prussia's Minister to the *Bundesrat*, the Confederation's Council – a position envisaged for a senior civil servant acting under direction. The constitution as eventually adopted made the Federal Chancellor the responsible director of the Confederation's entire policy, a circumstance which compelled Bismarck to assume that post himself. Henceforward he was wearing two hats: he was simultaneously Prussian Minister President and Federal Chancellor of the North German Confederation. Four years later the Federal Chancellor of the North German Confederation became the Reich Chancellor of the German Empire. Then, if not before, it became obvious that of the two offices that of the Chancellor had become the more important, and that Bismarck, without intending to do so, or indeed clearly realizing what he was doing, had in effect subordinated Prussia.

The North German Confederation did not yet call itself 'Reich' (even though it already possessed a north German 'Reichstag'), and the King of Prussia as the head of the North German Con-federation was not yet an Emperor but an impersonal neutral abstraction, the 'Presidium'. These 'insignificant-sounding but far-reaching expressions' were still, up to a point, obscuring the fact that, in a sense, every Prussian from now on possessed two state citizenships: a lesser Prussian and a greater North German (four years later German) one. He elected two parliaments: a Prussian Diet under a three-class electoral law and a North German (later a German) Reichstag on the basis of universal equal suffrage. When he was doing his military service he in fact served in two armies: the Prussian army and the federal army of which the Prussian army was now only one, though of course by far the biggest, constituent. An interesting point was also that decisions on the military budget were now, under the constitution of the North German Confederation, no longer made by the Prussian Diet but by the Reichstag – possibly the clearest indication of all that Prussia was in fact about to be absorbed in a larger political entity. What, after all, was left of Prussia if it could no longer determine the size of its own army?

So long as this was confined to the North German Confederation it was all more or less hidden by Prussia's enormous real preponderance over its small partners. But if one day the south German states were to join in, then this could not remain so any longer; what is more, Prussia's preponderance would then be appreciably reduced. Though even then Prussia would continue to be by far the greatest individual German state, it would still be only one individual state in a greatly enlarged entity. And that greater entity, no longer Prussia itself, would make the more important laws which regulated the life of every individual, and make the foreign policy decisions on which the destinies of the overall state – including the Prussian member state – depended. At the end of the road which Bismarck embarked upon by the foundation of the North German Confederation there could be nothing but the end of Prussian independence, Prussia's absorption into Germany.

We can be quite certain that Bismarck did not intend this – at least not until he became aware that it had turned into reality under his hands. Nor is there clear proof that he foresaw it. But many observations of the years between 1866 and 1870 suggest that he was in no hurry to promote German unity beyond the North German Confederation, and often one gains the impression that he found the prospect of wider German unity a little alarming, that some instinct caused him to hesitate. His instructions to the Prussian Minister in Munich in 1869 have become famous:

That German unity would be promoted by forcible events I, too, consider probable. But a very different matter is the avocation to bring about such a forcible catastrophe and responsibility for the choice of the moment. Any arbitrary and subjectively motivated intervention in the course of history has always only resulted in the knocking down of unripe fruit; and that German unity at this moment is not a ripe fruit, that in my opinion is obvious. . . . We may advance our clocks but time does not therefore move faster, and the ability to wait for conditions to develop is a prerequisite of practical politics.

That is not the language of a German national enthusiast. And there is at least one remark which offers a glimpse of the reason why Bismarck was inclined to shelve the enlargement of the North German Confederation into a German Empire with such philosophical calm. When Schleinitz, the Minister of the Royal Household, said to him: 'We must never go further than our supply of Prussian officers will stretch,' Bismarck replied: 'I cannot state so publicly but this is the basic idea of my entire policy.' If it really was that, then even the North German Confederation was a first step beyond that policy, and it becomes understandable that Bismarck should have shrunk from a second and bigger one.

Be that as it may, the idea that Bismarck during the years before 1870 had been systematically working towards the French war and the resulting foundation of the German Empire is a myth, though he himself helped to create it in his old age. The contrast between his policies before and after 1866 is striking: before, an almost hectic activity, a continuous deliberate pushing towards crisis, exacerbation and decision – and a clear goal. Afterwards came deliberate waiting and weighing, repeated avoidance of threatening crises, and a clear holding back from a closer association of northern Germany with southern Germany. In 1867 Bismarck put an end to the emerging risk of war with France over Luxembourg by a compromise that was highly unpopular with the German nationalists and included a Prussian withdrawal. In 1869 he declined an application of the Duchy of Baden for membership of the North German Confederation because he regarded it as a needless provocation of France. Even the Spanish succession candidature of a collateral Hohenzollern line, to which at the beginning of 1870 he persuaded the King, was not conceived by Bismarck as a war provocation – that may now be considered as certain in the light of the detailed research which, for over a century, has left no stone unturned – but, if anything, as a means of deterring France from warlike ventures. Bismarck referred to a 'Spanish peace fontanelle' which he wanted to keep open. Spain could never have been a threat to France; but – so Bismarck calculated – an uncertain Spain at its back might operate as a restraint on the French war party which, during the pre-1870 years, demanded 'revenge for Sadowa' and was trying to knock together an alliance with Austria and Italy. Bismarck in this instance decided on war only at the very last moment, when France, over-reacting, only left him the choice between war and humiliation. And even then he left the declaration of war to France.

The 1870–71 war, unlike the wars of 1864 and 1866, had not been sought by Bismarck or even allowed for beforehand; to him it was an accident and an improvisation, and for several months it slipped from his political control. A war which had started as an affair of honour between the Hohenzollern and Bonaparte dynasties turned into a German–French people's war. The elemental national hatreds which were released in it on both sides were fed more by memories of the days of the first Napoleon than by the cause of the war of 1870. To Bismarck they were a new and frightening phenomenon; suddenly it was no longer states who were fighting one another as in 1864 or 1866, but nations. To check this nationalist eruption, on both sides, now became Bismarck's problem, and it is against this background that both his foundation of the German Empire and his peace terms must be seen, especially the enforced surrender of Alsace-Lorraine to the newly founded German Reich. The two belong together. Both, to Bismarck, were precautions against a French war of revenge, a war which he was now expecting as a future certainty, following the boiling over of French national sentiments in the present war. Strangely enough, the decision to annex Alsace-Lorraine actually preceded his decision to establish the German Empire. One might almost say that the one entailed the other.

In 1867, at the time of the Luxembourg crisis, Bismarck had still declined to annex Alsace – and he did so with words which now have a prophetic ring about them: 'Even if the Prussians were victorious,' he had said, 'what would be the outcome? Even if one were to win Alsace one would have to maintain it; in the end the French would again find allies and then things might turn nasty!' It is certainly interesting that even at that time he had, almost automatically, equated victory over France with the annexation of Alsace (there was no question yet of Lorraine). He was always convinced that France would not forgive a defeat; and he was the more convinced of it since the cabinet war had developed into a people's war. But if a war of revenge had to be feared from France then the weak point of Prussia's defence was southern Germany. Bismarck was fond of quoting an earlier remark by the King of Württemberg: 'So long as Strasbourg is a gate for forays by a permanently armed power I must be in fear lest my country be swamped by foreign troops before . . . help can arrive.' Now Bismarck frequently called Strasbourg 'the key to our house', and if, as now seemed inevitable, France was to become an enemy for a long time, then he would rather have that key safely in his own pocket. That pocket, however, for reasons of geography, could not be a Prussian pocket. To enable Prussian troops to be stationed in Alsace-Lorraine they would have to be there on behalf of Germany. To annex Alsace-Lorraine – thus one thing entailed another – Bismarck needed a unified Germany.

But he also needed it in order to be sure of the south German states in the case of a French war of revenge. Neither in Bavaria nor in Württemberg, and still less so in Hesse-Darmstadt, had the monarchs or the governments been in a hurry, at the outbreak of the war in 1870, to meet their alliance obligations towards Prussia. Only an elemental eruption of hatred of the French (rather than love of Prussia) on the part of their people had eventually forced their hand. Bismarck had no wish, for a second time, to be dependent upon the shaky loyalty of the south German monarchs or on the south German popular mood. But in that case he had to swallow the bitter pill and go a great deal further than the supply of Prussian officers would stretch: he had to enlarge the North German Confederation into an all-German federal state, even if that meant a reduction in Prussian preponderance and new fuel for German nationalism which was now so alarmingly flaring up everywhere.

To channel that German nationalism, to keep it quiet, as it were, without letting it grow into a genuine force – that was one of Bismarck's principal aims. To Bismarck, German nationalism had been a useful ally of Prussia; it was certainly not his own cause. If circumstances were now compelling him to unify Germany he took care not to unify it too much. Within the new Germany there must be enough latitude for individual states to ensure that Prussia's preponderance should not be curtailed. Even at the time of the establishment of the North German Confederation Bismarck had once laid it down that 'we' (Prussians) would 'profit' if the confederal elements were not outweighed too much by the unavoidable federal-state elements of the new structure. He bore these considerations even more carefully in mind at the foundation of the Empire in 1871.

Hence his almost obsequious obligingness on the issue of special rights and reservations which were vigorously demanded by the south German states in the separate negotiations he conducted with them at Versailles. Of course they all realized that this accession amounted in effect to a loss of sovereignty, to subordination, and they resisted it with the innate self-preservation drive of any state organism. This suited Bismarck very well: the more independence was left to the south German states in the future all-German state, the more independence – and hence predominance – would Prussia be able to continue to exert. He conceded to the south German negotiators almost all their demands; Bavaria, in particular, nominally remained a virtually sovereign state, with its own army and its own diplomatic service; much to the outrage of the German nationalists who felt that

Bismarck might have extracted far more for German unity. But that was just what he did not want. He wanted a state in equilibrium, basically still a halfway entity between a federal state and a confederation of states; a Germany sufficiently united to stand together reliably in the event of war, and sufficiently disunited to consist, in peacetime, of recognizably separate states among which Prussia was the biggest, the most powerful, and the one that called the tune.

The final practical outcome of the negotiations at Versailles was nothing very exciting: an enlargement of the North German Confederation which, at the same time, meant a loosening of federal ties. One might almost speak of a closer North German and a looser all-German Confederation if one regarded only the constitutional outcome; and those who had looked forward to a genuinely unified Germany felt disappointed. 'She is an ugly wench but she will have to be married,' the National Liberal Deputy Lasker stated in the North German Reichstag. But now Bismarck had an inspired idea for sweetening the pill: he christened the 'ugly wench' fathered by him with the ancient venerable name 'German Reich', or German Empire, and he transformed the impersonal 'presidium' of the Confederation Council, a title held by the King of Prussia, into a 'German Emperor'.

'Kaiser and Reich', Emperor and Empire – those were concepts which made all hearts beat faster; they also killed several birds with one stone. These, after all, were the old demands of the Frankfurt National Assembly of 1848; to that extent, therefore, the democratic nationalists must feel satisfaction at seeing them implemented. But they were by no means, in origin, democratic or national concepts: the ancient Roman Empire of the German Nation had always been a loose association of princely states, anything but a national state, and the Emperor had been elected by the princes and not by the people. Even now Bismarck made quite sure that the imperial crown was offered to his King by the King's fellow princes (the King of Bavaria was won over by a massive bribe); the North German Reichstag was only permitted humbly to request the King not to reject the offer of the German princes. In this way 'Emperor and Empire' satisfied both the democrats and the princes. Besides, it struck a romantic chord in the people's sentiments – perhaps one should say it rang a bell. The new, prosaic and somewhat contradictory Prussian-German state structure was fitted with the halo of a resplendent thousand-year-old past, it presented itself as a resurrection of the legendary empire of Saxon and Staufen emperors. And finally the imperial title, to be henceforward hereditary in the Kings of Prussia, effectively emphasized the predominance which Bismarck was determined to preserve for his Prussia in the new Reich.

It was a stroke of genius, but at the same time paradoxical. Prussia as the founder of the Empire, considered historically, was almost as fantastic an idea as Luther becoming Pope. Let us recall the facts: the Kingdom of Prussia would not even have emerged if 'Prussia', that is to say East Prussia, had belonged to the Empire instead of to the Crown of Poland, and the Prussian King at first had been King only 'in' Prussia. Later, as King 'of' Prussia, he had been a perpetual thorn in the flesh of the Empire. Quite unlike Austria, which was deeply rooted in imperial history, had grown out of the Empire and had never been entirely separable from the idea of the Empire, Prussia was, if anything, a counter-foundation, an Anti-Empire. The Empire, ancient, weathered, towards its end scarcely definable in terms of constitutional law, had been a pan-European myth with its origins in ancient Rome. Prussia was as bright as a new penny, a purely rational state without any historical halo, entirely a power among powers, guided by nothing but statecraft, looking back not to the Middle Ages but to the Enlightenment. That Prussia should one day be the agent to renew the Empire would have been considered a joke by anyone in Prussia's classical era.

In 1871 it did seem at first as if 'Emperor and Empire' were only a pretty, old-German romantic-historical cloak for something entirely new and modern: for the German bourgeois national state. But we have seen that it was more than that: at least a divergence from the straightforward national state, a diversionary manoeuvre by which Bismarck had wanted to please everybody – princes as much as bourgeois nationalists, south Germans as much as north Germans, Prussians as much as non-Prussians – without giving any of them what they really and truly wanted.

For the moment at least he succeeded in doing just that, except for one person: his own King. To the aged Wilhelm I, Emperor and Empire, as he literally stated, meant a 'farewell to Prussia'. He predicted that the imperial title he was to bear forthwith would outshine the Prussian royal title. At the most he was prepared to be 'Emperor of Germany' in the way he had previously been King of Prussia – to see Germany absorbed into Prussia instead of Prussia into Germany. If that was not possible – 'What use is that character major to me?' ('character major' was the term used for captains who upon discharge from the service were given a major's rank as a consolation prize). At the last moment he even wanted to prevent his proclamation as Emperor and talked of abdication. ('Let Fritz do this business. He goes along with the new state of affairs with his entire soul. But I don't care a hoot about it and stick to Prussia.') When Bismarck – one day before his proclamation as Emperor – eventually got him to yield, as he always did, the King, bursting into tears, said: 'Tomorrow is the unhappiest day of my life. We shall be burying the Prussian Kingdom.'

Bismarck, in a letter to his wife, dismissed this as a quirky royal caprice, and most historians subsequently looked on it in much the same way: at best as an old man's sentimental weakness for the old and outdated. That is how most people saw it at the time, including most Prussians. But the old King saw further than most. The imperial proclamation at Versailles on 18 January 1871, 170 years to the day after the coronation of the first Prussian King in Königsberg, was the beginning of Prussia's slow death.

7

THE SLOW DEMISE

Revolution of Consciousness – Rearguard Actions – An Unwanted State – Prussia's Extinction

PRUSSIA CONTINUED TO EXIST within the German Reich for another seventy-five years, even though as a mere shadow at the end of the period, and it only perished in 1945 together with the Reich. But Reich history and Prussian history throughout this three-quarter century are not identical and indeed not even parallel; if anything they run in opposite directions. The Reich flourished and became increasingly powerful; Prussia declined and became increasingly impotent as part of the Reich. The history of the German Reich between 1871 and 1945 is an exciting, dramatic, grand and terrible spectacle; Prussian history of that period is a mere epilogue of Prussian history proper, an irreversible decline into provincialism. Germany, until it literally burst apart in 1945, had made the whole world hold its breath throughout six frightful years; during those six years no one was in the least interested in Prussia; even to its own inhabitants it was no longer a living reality. It had been absorbed into Germany, just as King Frederick Wilhelm IV had predicted in a clear-sighted moment in 1848.

But how was that possible? Surely the German Reich had been a Prussian foundation? Had not Prussia in 1871 become the dominating power in Germany? Had it not, in Bismarck's Empire, held in its hand all the trump cards, so completely that the Germany of the day had been frequently referred to as 'Greater Prussia'? How had it come about that all those trump cards in the end failed to win the tricks, that Prussia, instead of dominating Germany, increasingly lost itself, without resistance, and finally dissolved into Germany? Precisely when had all that happened? In 1890, when Bismarck went? In 1918, when the monarchy came to an end? In 1932, when the Prussian Government was deposed by the Reich Government? Or only during the succeeding years, with the appointment of Reich Governors and the rechristening of the German states into *Reichsgaue*?

All these events and dates undoubtedly mark stages in what has rightly been called Prussia's post-history, but it cannot be asserted that they represent decisive turning-points at which events could have taken a different course. Each stage merely recorded something that had already happened; the lack of resistance to the course of events and the sense of inevitability which accompanied them – these invariably proved that the Prussian state had merely lost another part of its vitality. Each new loss of power was only another stage in a process of slow and relentless dying. And if we now ask at what moment this uncanny, unnoticed process began and what had caused it, then there is only one answer. The decisive event which severed Prussia's vital nerve can only have been the establishment of the Reich – that supreme triumph of Prussia that seemed to be making Prussia the heart of Germany. In the long run it turned out that Prussia, in spite of all power-political appearances and all Bismarckian constitutional precautions, was not strong enough to survive its fusion with Germany. Like the man whose heart is carried off by Rilke's angel, 'it expired from its stronger existence'.

Anyone thinking that this sounds too mystical should remember Hegel's famous dictum: 'Once the realm of imagination has been revolutionized reality will not stand up.' True, the reality which Bismarck had created in Germany in 1871 clearly favoured Prussia. The King of Prussia was German Emperor, Prussia dominated the *Bundesrat*, it provided the Reich Chancellor, it elected the largest number of Reichstag members and not only supplied the core of the Reich's armed forces but also reformed the armies of the other German countries on the Prussian model. Any German doing his military service had 'gone to the Prussians' – one of those popular turns of phrase which reveal an instinctive grasp of complicated constitutional arrangements (nowadays the young German serviceman goes 'to the Federation'). In constitutional reality Bismarck's Reich was something halfway between a federal state and a confederation of states in which Prussia was, both politically and militarily, clearly the dominating power.

At the same time, however, Bismarck, without quite realizing what he was doing, had revolutionized 'the realm of the imagination'. In the imagination of the Germans the German Reich was their long-hoped-for national state; moreover the high-sounding words 'Emperor and Empire' awakened ancient deeply buried ideas of universal power and greatness. In the common German consciousness Prussia, by founding the German Reich, had discharged its historical task and fulfilled its 'German mission'. For that it deserved gratitude, but by that it had also become superfluous. It no longer had a *raison d'être*, it had been outstripped as an independent state, it had become a thing of yesterday, a glorious chunk of German history, something that one would regard in future as one does a museum exhibit or a prize cup in a display case.

And this revolutionizing of the consciousness had occurred not only in non-Prussian Germany but above all in Prussia itself. After all, the Prussians, at least in their overwhelming majority, were also Germans; and their German national sentiments, now that they had found a focus by the foundation of the Reich, proved far superior in strength and depth to their ancient Prussian loyalties. This happened especially, of course, in the new 'compulsorily Prussian', territories of western and northwestern Germany which had not been taken over by Prussia until 1815 or even 1866 and which had not shared, as Prussians, in the most glorious periods of Prussia's history; but it also happened in the ancient Prussian territories. Berlin, for instance, was now proud of its new title of 'Reich capital'. That in addition it continued to be the capital of the Kingdom of Prussia and residence of its King it was scarcely aware of any longer. Indeed it has to be faced that Munich, Stuttgart and Dresden – and with them the countries they represented – preserved far more local provincial and tribal awareness than Berlin or Prussia.

If one reflects for a moment this is understandable enough: the

Prussians, just because they had founded this Empire and now regarded themselves as its real exponents, were more readily and more easily prepared to identify totally with it – 'their' Reich – and, as it were, forget their separate statehood. After all, they were not a tribe like the Bavarians, the Swabians or the Saxons; tribal awareness, less strongly marked than in southern Germany, existed at best in the Prussian provinces, amongst East Prussians, Silesians, Pomeranians and Brandenburgers. But Prussia as Prussia had never had a tribal basis any more than it had had a national one; it had always been a pure state, an artificial structure of power and reason, one to which one belonged by accident or by an act of will ('I am a Prussian, I wish to be a Prussian!' said a patriotic Prussian song), but not because nature had created one a Prussian in the way it had created one a German or even a Bavarian or a Saxon. If that brittle artificial rational state was now restricting itself by, as it were, superimposing a second greater state, the German Reich, upon itself, then it was hardly surprising if its inhabitants' sense of Prussian statehood was quickly overshadowed by their newly aroused German national patriotism. To be a Prussian had always been a sober business, a matter of obedience, correct behaviour and fulfilment of duty. But to be allowed to be a German, and now even a subject of the German Emperor and a citizen of a German Reich, was something enthralling and intoxicating. 'Deutschland, Deutschland über alles' – the song had existed even before Germany became a political reality. To sing 'Preussen über alles' had never occurred to anyone.

This change in consciousness – which was never 'news', never an 'event', and yet was an epoch-making process – was taking place not only among the people but also greatly involved the state-supporting classes, the politicians, civil servants and ministers, and indeed the ruling house. Wilhelm I had foreseen it with pain at the time of the imperial proclamation at Versailles, and he would have preferred to remain a simple King of Prussia. Now, in spite of everything, he became the 'old Emperor' and submitted to his new greater and unwanted role with a Prussian sense of duty. His son, the eternal Crown Prince, was already totally absorbed in the German Empire; when, in 1888, terminally sick, he succeeded to the throne for a brief three months, he only wished to be called the 'Emperor Frederick', and not 'Frederick III' because that would have pointed to his secondary Prussian title. And Wilhelm II, eventually, was quite simply 'the Kaiser', the Emperor. That he was also King of Prussia and that Prussia was still a state in the Reich and alongside the Reich – indeed the dominant state – had become a totally nebulous idea to him. In the summer of 1892 Wilhelm II made a significant observation on this subject to his favourite Eulenburg, who recorded it: 'I still don't quite understand a remark which Prince Bismarck made to me on one occasion. Its intent is not clear to me, and there is always some intent dormant behind his thoughts. He said: "With the German Reich things are merely so-so. All you need to do is try to make Prussia strong. It doesn't matter what becomes of the rest." I regarded this as a kind of trap for me.'

It was not a trap. Bismarck, as so often, had uttered with startling and bewildering frankness what he really thought and felt. The founder of the Reich – almost he alone – had remained a Prussian, body and soul. To him the German Reich was not an end in itself but an intricate arrangement for the enlargement of Prussia's power position beyond Prussia's state frontiers; and, viewed thus, the arrangement could soon be described as 'merely so-so'.

In order to achieve his purpose Bismarck had entered into two mutually contradictory and not quite sincere alliances: one with the German territorial princes, to whom he left a sham sovereignty complete with monarchical titles and court splendour in order to make their actual subordination to Prussia more palatable to them; and the other with 'the German people', with liberal and democratic German nationalism to which he conceded the great objectives of 1848, Emperor and Empire, and moreover a freely elected German Reichstag – for which, admittedly, he had envisaged no more than a gratefully acclamatory role. With the princes everything had gone more or less smoothly. But the German people and the German Reichstag sadly disappointed Bismarck's expectations. Instead of being grateful they were demanding.

Where Bismarck had intended to offer them the little finger they eagerly seized the whole hand.

His King and Emperor, with whom he had had such difficult wrangles in the early years, later gave Bismarck no trouble and even the often complained of regional 'particularism' of the southern Germans was only a surface problem – no matter how much the Bavarians ranted about those *Saupreussen*, those bloody Prussians, there was never any danger of a Bavarian secession. It was the Reichstag that Bismarck the Prussian soon found truly frightening. That freely elected German parliament from the very outset totally eclipsed the Prussian Diet which was elected publicly and indirectly under a three-class electoral law. Time and again the Reich Chancellor had to face the Reichstag and conduct exhausting debates, and, in consequence, Bismarck the Prussian Minister President was increasingly overshadowed by Bismarck the Reich Chancellor – much to his displeasure. It was in the Reichstag that the change of consciousness which we have mentioned found its most articulate expression, that replacement of a specifically Prussian sense of statehood by an overwhelming sense of German nationality. Bismarck sensed this, without being able to name this elusive opponent. Indeed, time and again, he had to pay lip service to it in order not to jeopardize his alliance, or sham-alliance, with German nationalism.

Instead he attacked what he called the 'party spirit' which, after all, was no more than the natural expression of an increasingly vigorous national democracy. Reich Chancellor Bismarck's two great domestic fights were with the two big German national parties which presently emerged in the Reich, the Catholic Centre Party and the Social Democratic Party of Germany. He called them 'enemies of the Reich'. In fact they were the real Reich parties and – the Centre Party having expanded in an inter-denominationally Christian way to become the CDU, the Christian Democratic Union – have remained so to this day. Bismarck's attempt at paralysing them – the Centre Party by the *Kulturkampf*, the State–Church conflict, and the SPD by his anti-socialist legislation – made the seventies and eighties resound with the din of domestic political strife; they were the unattractive principal internal policy issues of the Bismarck era. Both of them also yielded something useful: the *Kulturkampf* civil marriage and the abolition of ecclesiastical supervision over education; the struggle against the SPD the epoch-making invention of social insurance. But in the final political outcome they were both of them defeats for Bismarck. The Centre Party and the Social Democrats did not become weaker but grew ever stronger. This double defeat explains why Bismarck, shortly before his dismissal, was quite seriously considering the dissolution of the Reich and its re-establishment as a pure alliance of princes, involving the abolition of the Reichstag or at least of the Reichstag electoral law.

The internal atmosphere of Bismarck's Reich during its first twenty years was unpleasant and stuffy, and Bismarck himself, at the peak of his power and fame, became increasingly bitter. His Prussian calculations had misfired in the establishment of the Reich; the Reich, instead of becoming a Greater Prussia, was developing an un-Prussian life of its own, overshadowing Prussia. Bismarck tried to resist this, stubbornly and inventively – also brutally – but in vain. His creation was stronger than he was. At any rate, so long as Bismarck existed Prussia also still existed. Bismarck's internal policy between 1871 and 1890 may be reduced to a simple formula: it was the last manifestation of Prussia's refusal to be absorbed into Germany – a vain refusal. It was Prussia's last, prolonged and unsuccessful rearguard action.

Few people have praised Bismarck's domestic policy after 1871; on the other hand his foreign policy has found all the more eulogists. As is well known, Bismarck amazed the world when, after eight years of turbulent politics in a Bonapartist style, full of crises and ever ready for war, he became a paragon of peace. Throughout twenty years he preserved and cultivated the peace of Europe with the same painstaking coolly calculating mastery – one might even say with the same passion – with which he had earlier pursued Prussia's aggrandisement and the solution of the German problem in a Prussian sense. On one occasion, in 1878, he prevented an imminent major European war as an 'honest broker'; and he always insisted that there was nothing left that the German Reich had to 'conquer by the sword'. 'We are a saturated state.' When he used the expression 'we' Bismarck, without actually saying so, invariably meant 'Prussia', and if one blames the unattractive aspects of his domestic policy on his obstinate Prussian allegiance then surely the merits of his foreign policy should also be credited to the same source.

Prussia after 1871 was indeed a saturated and a more than saturated state; there was indeed nothing left for Prussia to conquer by the sword. It had already swallowed more than it could digest, it was sated and oversated, and its interest now was nothing more than peace and quiet. For Prussia, to quote Bismarck again, 'the German clock was now correctly set for a hundred years'; the foundation of the Empire – another Bismarck quotation – was 'the most that "we" could expect Europe to accept'. The Prussian interest, the real lodestar of Bismarck's policy throughout his life, therefore, while Bismarck held the office of Reich Chancellor, acted as a brake on the foreign policy of the Reich. Since Prussia was saturated the Reich, too, had to act as a saturated state, which in fact it was not. And this emerged clearly as soon as Bismarck departed. As a national state the German Reich was not saturated because millions of Germans were still outside it; and as an Empire – that is as a newly fledged great power and the secret predominant power in Europe – there was no telling where it would find the limits to its ambitions; 'world power' and 'world politics' were concepts already knocking at its door, and 'living space' was only two generations away. So long as Bismarck – and through Bismarck Prussia – determined Germany's foreign policy all this was still kept under strict control. Prussia found the German Reich, as created in 1871, sufficient: hence the German Reich itself had better content itself with what had been created so far. That was the inner logic of Bismarck's peace policy, a policy soon abandoned after his departure. This peace policy of the German Reich during its first twenty years was essentially still Prussian policy.

A great many foreign historians, above all English but also some southern German and Austrian historians, have refused to accept this. To them Prussia was 'the root of all evil', Germany's evil spirit and the real cause of the disasters into which Germany precipitated itself and the world during the first half of the twentieth century. They support their views by two plausible-sounding arguments.

For one thing, the principal instrument of the German Reich in the two world wars of the twentieth century had been its army, and that army – this is entirely correct – had essentially been the product of Prussia and of 'Prussian militarism'. But it was not the army which determined German policy prior to the two world wars or which urged war; indeed, in the case of the Second World War, it earnestly advised against it.

For another thing, the argument continues, Prussia during its history as an independent state, and especially in the eighteenth but once again in the second third of the nineteenth century, had been a conquering state; time and again it had pursued a policy of aggrandisement and expansion – and that tradition of conquest it had passed on, or, as it were, inoculated into, the German Reich founded by it. The first part of this argument is entirely correct, except that it omits the fact that a policy of territorial expansion was universal practice in the eighteenth century and that Prussia, because of its prolonged territorial disjointedness, depended on it more than anyone else. But the second and decisive part of the argument is pure fantasy. Prussia never 'passed on' anything to or 'inoculated' anything into the German Reich. With the foundation of the Reich in 1871 it had reached the goal and the end of its career. Indeed, with the foundation of the Reich it had even exceeded the uttermost limits of its expandability. And so long as Prussia had any say in the Reich at all – until Bismarck's departure – it always was the conservative, stabilizing, retarding and peace-preserving element in German foreign policy. Not, by any means, from pacifism, but from its soberly assessed state interests. If it wanted to remain the leading power in Germany – and under Bismarck it did want to be that – Germany must on no account grow any bigger than it was already. Prussia could not even truly 'dominate' Germany such as it was; even in Bismarck's lesser German Reich it suddenly, much to its alarm, found itself perpetually on the defensive, indeed in the position of the proverbial man riding a tiger. In a Greater Germany or in a German 'world power' its position would have become even more hopeless. Bismarck realized that and yet even he was no longer able to prevent the consequences. In foreign policy, too, his creation was eventually more powerful than himself. After all, there was no such thing as Prussian foreign policy after 1871. Prussia no longer was an independent entity under international law – that was now the German Reich, and that German Reich, whether Bismarck liked it or not, was something different from and bigger than Prussia had been: not a northeast European regional state with limited and easily seen interests but a great power with interests throughout Europe and very soon beyond.

This emerged for the first time during the great Balkan crisis between Russia and Britain which threatened to precipitate Europe into a general war in 1878. The Congress which settled it met in Berlin, with Bismarck as President, and the peace terms depended upon him as the 'honest broker'. The German Reich had become the arbitrator of Europe – a proud part which Prussia could never have played or would even have wished to play, and in which, of course, there was no room for Prussian policy. Bismarck the peacemaker had to stay the hand of a victorious Russia; and that was the end of a hundred years of Prussian–Russian friendship and the beginning of German–Russian enmity which, likewise, was to have a history of almost a hundred years. It soon compelled Bismarck to take the next step: the alliance with Austria, that most un-Prussian of all alliances, yet one from which the German Reich was never to extricate itself again.

Similarly un-Prussian was the colonial policy to which Bismarck was most reluctantly persuaded in the eighties, under the pressure of German overseas enterprises and a 'social-imperialist' propaganda which believed that colonies were the way out of a serious economic depression. None of this had anything to do with Prussia or Prussian interests. But Germany had simply become more powerful than Prussia, even under Bismarck, who still thought in Prussian terms and tried to put a brake on 'his'

Germany. After his departure there was no one left to put a brake on Germany; the slogan now was 'Full steam ahead!'

German history, as is well known, becomes most exciting under Wilhelm II, a highly dramatic history of splendour and misery, high flying and crashing – but we are not concerned here with German but with Prussian history, and this is why, with the onset of the Wilhelmian era, we find ourselves in difficulties: suddenly there is no such thing left as genuine Prussian history. What used to be Prussian history and what, even in Bismarck's Reich, had still represented a certain counterpoint to German history, declines into insignificant provincial history in the period between 1890 and 1914. This does not mean that Prussia, more particularly the West German new Prussia, where the big and now flourishing German industrial regions were situated, was excluded from the tremendous upsurge of power in Wilhelm's Germany: industrial expansion, the naval construction programme, 'world politics'. It is simply that none of this has anything to do with Prussia, with the Prussian state or with Prussian traditions. If indeed there is anything of significance to report on the Prussia of that period, then it is a strange process of secret regression and internal splitting and splintering. The Prussian state's well-tested power of integration was clearly declining. The west German neo-Prussians enthusiastically shared in the upswing of the Wilhelm period; they felt liberated and endowed with new wings. But in 'Old Prussia', the Prussia of 1772, the land of Junkers and peasants east of the Elbe, a land that suddenly found itself reduced to the status of a poor relation in the new industrialized Germany, memories were being revived of an outdated birthright, a cult of one's ancient character began, and there was much offended grumbling and snarling about that neo-German character, the ostentation, the wealth, the worldly ambition. Even the Kaiser, who had so patently forgotten that he should really be a King of Prussia, was not spared from this Junker criticism. And it was understandable. There was indeed a great deal of unattractive, newly-rich boastfulness and ostentation in the Germany of Wilhelm II, which contrasted unfavourably with old Prussian modesty and solidity. The Prussian

Junker officers and peasant soldiers had once upon a time set up a remarkable state, and but for that state there would have been no German Reich, the Reich which had now so haughtily overtaken it. How had it all come about? Was the Prussian Minister President not to have been the Reich Chancellor on the side? Now suddenly the Reich Chancellor was Prussian Minister President on the side – and indeed he might be a Bavarian such as Prince Hohenlohe, or a Mecklenburgian such as Bülow, or the scion of a Frankfurt family such as Bethmann-Hollweg, or another Bavarian such as Hertling, or indeed a member of the ruling house of Baden such as Prince Max. Yes, it was quite true : the old Prussia, 'East Elbia' – the term now emerged – had, within the German Reich which after all owed it its own existence, become a backwoods region within a few decades, a province, 'farmland' – and, moreover, subsidized by the Reich. Its grain production could only be made to pay through high protective tariffs which increased the price the West German industrial worker had to pay for his bread, and nevertheless the East-Elbian estates were deep in debt. Poor old Prussia!

Clearly this Old-Prussian disenchantment with the Reich during the Wilhelmian era is entirely understandable, and later, in the light of the collapse of 1918, it was even seen as a kind of superior wisdom. If only the Reich had remained as modest as Prussia! But it is often overlooked that this latter-day Prussian criticism also contains a good deal of un-Prussian self-pity, a lot of egoism and a certain obduracy. Not all was sham, and not all the new life that was stirring in the German Reich of that period – economically, culturally and also politically – was bad. In view of the freer and broader development of German life during the quarter-century from 1890 to 1914 the perpetual grumpy complaints heard from East-Elbia seem not so much the voice of a prophet warning against disaster as a symptom of Prussian decadence. After all, what was one to think of a Prussia which, at a time when all other German states were adopting universal equal suffrage, was stubbornly clinging to its outdated and hated three-class electoral law dating from the 1850s? And was that eternal self-reflection and self-admiration, something Prussia never knew in its better days, not at least equally bad form as the Wilhelm era's glitter and ostentation? 'Our upper class,' Theodor Fontane wrote with gentle mockery in 1898, 'has a naive tendency to regard anything "Prussian" as a higher form of culture.'

Theodor Fontane was and remains Prussia's classical poet. Not properly a German but of predominantly French blood, a descendant of the French colony which ever since the days of the Great Elector had been at home in Prussia, he was a Prussian through and through. In his youth he was Prussia's bard, in his manhood the chronicler of Prussia's wars, victories and history – there is no finer historical novel in the German language, none more worth reading and loving, than his *Before the Storm*, a book whose real hero is the land of Prussia. Fontane in his old age became a clear-sighted, sad and incorruptible critic of Prussian decadence:

The 'Non soli cedo' eagle with its bundle of lightning flashes in its claws, flashes no longer and enthusiasm is dead. A reverse movement now exists, things long dead are to flower anew – but they do not. . . . The ancient families are still popular, even today. But they squander and bury those sympathies which, surely, everyone needs, every individual and every class. Our ancient families all suffer from the belief 'that nothing can be done without them', which is far from the truth; things are certainly possible without them; they are no longer the main supporting pillar, they are the old stone and moss roof which still weighs heavily and presses down but no longer affords protection against bad weather.

This passage comes from Fontane's last and greatest novel, *Stechlin*, a valedictory work in every sense. It is also Fontane's valediction to Prussia.

The age of Wilhelm II, for Germany an age of springtime and upsurge, was for Prussia an autumnal period of farewell; Prussia was in decline, and when the German thrones collapsed in 1918 – soundlessly and unresistingly, thereby setting the seal upon their non-restorability – it seemed for a moment as if Prussia had finally come to an end.

We skip the First World War since it was not a Prussian war.

Austria, Russia, Germany, France, Britain and America, who entered the war in this order, all had their reasons for war and their war aims. Prussia had none. Yet Prussia paid the price of Germany's defeat. With the exception of Alsace-Lorraine all German territorial surrenders were at Prussia's expense: Posen and Upper Silesia, Danzig and the Polish 'corridor', even North Schleswig. And the German revolution which followed defeat confronted Prussia with a life-and-death issue.

This was not only because this was a predominantly West German revolution which did not engulf Berlin until the very end and which never occurred at all in 'East-Elbia' proper, but mainly because Prussia, by losing the Hohenzollern dynasty, had lost the principal ligature which until then had held the state together. Bismarck, a Prussian also in this respect, in his *Thoughts and Reminiscences*, put forward the thesis that it was not the tribes but the dynasties which were the foundations of the separate German states and of the inevitable German federalism. This, as far as Bavaria, Württemberg, Saxony, and others are concerned, is a highly questionable thesis; but it is true of Prussia. The years 1918–19 showed that in all other German states a vigorous awareness of identity remained alive even without their 'traditional' dynasties. Only Prussia became a problem without its King, indeed an embarrassing problem. Suddenly, in a sense, it no longer knew what to do with itself; it was now quite ready to ratify even formally its absorption into Germany, an absorption which in the consciousness of most of its inhabitants had already silently taken place during the imperial era.

The Prussian Constituent Assembly, which had been elected simultaneously with the Weimar National Assembly in January 1919 – now of course by universal equal vote – hesitated for a long time about tackling its task. What was the point of a Prussian constitution alongside the German? Why have a Prussia at all now that one had Germany? Even in December 1919 – one year after the revolution and four months after the coming into force of the Weimar Reich Constitution – the Prussian Assembly, by 210 against 32 votes, passed a Resolution whose vital sentences read:

As the largest of the German states Prussia considers it its duty first of all to make the attempt at creating, at this time, a unified German state. On the grounds of these considerations the Assembly requests the State Government immediately and even before the enactment of the final constitution to induce the Reich Government to enter into negotiations with the Governments of all German constituent states about the establishment of a unified German state.

Prussia thus was prepared to dissolve itself – but none of the other German states was, and hence nothing came of the unified German state. Prussia, whether it liked it or not, had to learn to live with its continued existence as a state though fundamentally it no longer wanted it.

There were in 1919 also other plans for the dissolution of Prussia, aiming not at a unified German state but at a German federal republic. In a federal state a member such as Prussia, which alone was larger than all the other states, in a sense a duplication of the overall state on a reduced scale, was a striking anomaly. If federalism was to be adopted then it would have been reasonable to divide Prussia into three or four handy, tribally more or less homogeneous German states of roughly the size of Bavaria – as in fact has happened with the western parts of Prussia in the present Federal Republic. Adenauer, then Lord Mayor of Cologne, made such a proposal for the Rhineland at the beginning of 1919: it would secede from Prussia – but not from the Reich. The first draft of the Weimar Constitution also envisaged the division of Prussia into several new states.

But that the Prussians would not have. Absorption into a unified German state seemed honourably in line with the times; but to be sub-divided into Rhinelanders, Westphalians, Lower Saxons and East-Elbians ran counter to an inherited instinct; that was not what the Prussian Kings had worked for, toiled for and waged wars for throughout two centuries. Thus the republican Prussians – Social Democrats, Centre Party and Liberals, the majority of the Constituent Assembly and the subsequent Diets – half reluctantly (they would have preferred a unified German state) and half stubbornly (they did not want to see Prussia partitioned) – assumed the inheritance of the Prussian

Kings. The curtain was rung up on the final act of Prussian post-history.

As befits the final act of a well-constructed tragedy it produced one more 'moment of final tension', one deceptive hope that everything might perhaps still turn out well. Republican Prussia surprisingly became the model state of Republican Germany. Unlike the Weimar Reich which in fourteen years ran through thirteen Reich Chancellors and never settled down under its continually changing coalition governments, Prussia during the Weimar period was governed, with but one brief interruption, throughout the period of 1920 to 1932 by the same Minister President, and he governed well. The East Prussian Otto Braun, 'the last King of Prussia', was undoubtedly the strongest political talent and the strongest political personality among the German Social Democrats of the Weimar Republic. He kept his party and its coalition – always the same coalition – strictly in order, he won all his electoral campaigns, he made Prussia crisis-proof (while in the Reich one crisis was succeeding another), and he introduced a number of reforms which in their day were epoch-making, such as the famous Prussian educational reform of 1921 and, a few years later, an equally liberal reform of Prussian penal practice. Far more so than the Weimar Republic, the republican Prussia of the twenties appears to us as a precursor or a model of the present-day Federal Republic: a first proof that even Germans can sensibly handle republican institutions and democratic freedoms. One odd fact is that Otto Braun's Prussia made an entirely original political discovery at the last moment, one which has since become a constitutional cornerstone of stability in the Federal Republic: the constructive vote of no confidence – the stipulation that a parliament can overthrow a head of government only by electing another.

The idea was of course born of necessity, as are most good ideas. In 1932 elections were due in Prussia, and it was easy to foresee that the National Socialists and Communists jointly would have a majority – a majority which could unseat the government but would be unable to produce a joint alternative government. Foreseeing this contingency the Braun Government, as the last act of the Prussian Diet's legislative period expiring in 1932, introduced the constructive vote of no confidence and it is not inconceivable that, if conditions in the Reich had been otherwise, this might have enabled it to survive the Nazi surge. The government was eventually overthrown not by the Prussian Diet but by the 'Prussian *coup d'état*' of Reich Chancellor Papen of 20 July 1932.

This date marks the real end of the Prussian state. On that day the Reich Chancellor, with full powers from the Reich President, deposed the Prussian State Government and appointed himself 'Reich Commissar for Prussia'. The Prussian Ministries were occupied by the Reichswehr and the Ministers invited, under threat of force, to leave their offices. They yielded to the invitation. Resistance was not attempted. A Prussian complaint to the Reich Court yielded no decisive result. On 20 July 1932 Prussia virtually acquired a status similar to that of Alsace-Lorraine between 1871 and 1918; it became a 'Reich *Land*' governed, without a government of its own, by the Reich Government as it were with its left hand. That was the end of its existence as a separate state – the end of Prussia.

It was, when all is said and done, a miserable end – not only of the short but respectable republican final period of Prussia but of Prussian history generally. Whether the Prussian Government might not, or should not, have shaped it a little more heroically, whether it should not have faced force with force – on that point a great deal of argument went on at the time and still goes on. Otto Braun and his Minister of the Interior, the Westphalian Carl Severing, until their deaths stuck to the view that their unheroic behaviour was reasonable and correct. Resistance, Otto Braun wrote in his memoirs long after 1945, would have meant not only civil war but also a bloody defeat. The Prussian police were no match for the Reichswehr, and probably not psychologically ready to engage the Reichswehr in armed conflict; as for the workers, they had no weapons. A general strike, at a time when there were six million unemployed, was out of the question. This all sounds very reasonable. But there still remains the impression of an inglorious surrender – to a plot which surely contained an unmistakable measure of bluff. After all, Papen was not in a strong position either. The Reichswehr was no more ready for a civil war than the Prussian police, and would probably have dropped Papen at the first hint of civil war, just as, a few months later, it actually did when he suggested it.

But the oddest thing of all – and for Prussia's self-surrender without a fight probably the decisive element – was the fact that in the consciousness of the actors and observers at the time the state of Prussia was no longer at issue. Surely that state had been ready twelve years earlier to be absorbed in a unified German state; it had become a problem to itself, it had lost any will to assert itself as a state *vis-à-vis* the Reich. To the Prussians of 1932 the issue on 20 July was no longer essentially Prussia as such. To them Papen's Prussian *coup d'état* was merely a move in the triangular struggle between Republicans, German Conservative Nationalists and National Socialists for power in the Reich. That was the great issue of 1932, and to contemporaries the fall of the Republican bastion of Prussia was, above all, a victory of the conservative party: by razing the Social Democratic fortress of Prussia Papen dealt a direct blow to the Republicans, and an indirect one also to the National Socialists; he strengthened the German conservatives who were then hoping to be the winners in the quarrel between the right-wing and left-wing popular parties, and so to re-establish upper-class rule.

What was especially confusing was that throughout the Weimar period the German nationalists had appropriated the term 'Prussia' as though Prussia had always been a German national institution, and they had used 'Prussia' as a banner and as a stick to beat the Republic with. A grotesque election poster of those years shows a bleeding heart with the caption: 'The Prussian heart! Who can heal it? The German National People's Party!' Under the same heading come the questionable Prussian myth-making activities of men like Spengler and Moeller van den Bruck in the twenties and, on a lower level, the Fridericus Rex films of the Hugenberg Ufa concern which cleverly misrepresented the King of Prussia as a nationalist and reactionary propaganda figure. The climax and termination of that German nationalist swindle about Prussia was the embarrassing 'Potsdam Day' on 21 March 1933, the solemn inaugural meeting of the newly elected Reichstag under the newly elected Reich Chancellor Hitler, an event that was to set the seal on the short-lived and to the conservative German nationalists disastrous alliance between Papen and Hitler. That alliance was dressed up on that Potsdam Day as an alliance between Prussian tradition and National Socialist revolution. The Potsdam Garrison Church had to provide the stage setting, the German national *Stahlhelm* organization marched alongside the National Socialist storm troopers, the Reichswehr provided the walk-ons, and the ancient Reich President Hindenburg, who as a young Prussian lieutenant had taken part in the Battle of Königgrätz, was allowed in his speech to refer to 'the old Prussia'. This in no way changed the fact that Prussia presently disappeared almost without trace in Hitler's Reich. The Bavarian Göring, among the numerous titles which he collected, did, it is true, also bear that of a Prussian Minister President. But no political function was associated with it. No separate Prussian role can be detected in Hitler's Reich even with a magnifying glass.

Does one seriously have to deal once more with the foolish theory that Hitler's Reich was a continuation of Prussian traditions and Hitler the heir to Frederick the Great and Bismarck? No one who has taken the trouble to read thus far requires an elaborate refutation. Just a few brief words. Prussia, whatever else it may have been, was a state based on law, one of the first in Europe. But the rule of law was the first thing that Hitler abolished. In its racial and nationality policy Prussia had always displayed noble toleration and indifference. Hitler's racial and nationality policy was the extreme opposite of Prussia's. So was Hitler's political style the extreme opposite of Prussian soberness – his demagogy and theatrical intoxication of the masses. And if German history has any connecting link at all with Hitler's foreign policy, with his megalomaniac ideas of conquest, then that link was not a Prussian but an Austrian one: Schwarzenberg's policy of 1850, his vision of a vast empire in central Europe. Hitler, after all, was an Austrian and the joke that made the round of

Berlin in the thirties was not far off the mark: 'Hitler is Austria's revenge for Königgrätz.'

On the other side the attempt has also occasionally been made to credit to Prussian traditions and attitudes the German conservative opposition to Hitler – which ran like some subterranean stream through the whole twelve years of the Third Reich and eventually, for a brief moment, emerged in the light of day – to let Prussia's history end not with the inglorious 20th of July 1932 but with another, more glorious, 20th of July: the attempted conservative *putsch* of 1944. But this, on closer examination, is not tenable either. It is true that the list of victims of that *putsch* contains many great Prussian names: a Yorck and a Moltke, a Hardenberg and a Schulenburg, a Kleist and a Schwerin, to name but a few. But the principal character on 20 July 1944, Stauffenberg, was a Bavarian, and all the other German tribes had their representatives among those who, in this belated and unsuccessful rescue attempt, staked and mostly lost their lives. What those men tried to save was not Prussia but Germany. For them, too, Prussia had long been absorbed into Germany; in their political plans and drafts for a united and renewed Germany Prussia no longer played any part, and even if they had been successful Prussia would not have risen again. Even to the Prussians among them their former state had become a mere memory.

All that is left now is a glance at the final and most frightful chapter of Prussian post-history. This no longer concerns the Prussian state; that no longer existed. It was not Prussia as Prussia that paid the price of the lost Second World War, as it had done of the First; but the Prussian people did so, East Prussians and West Prussians, Pomeranians, people from the New Mark, and Silesians, those people of mixed German and Western Slav blood who had once provided the principal part of Prussia's national substance. They lost the land which throughout seven centuries had been their homeland – first through mass escape and later through expulsion. Thus the Prussian tree now also had its roots dug up long after its foliage had withered and its trunk been felled. What these expulsions reversed and, as it were, revoked was no longer Prussian history: it was the very origin of Prussian prehistory, the colonial history of the twelfth and thirteenth centuries, the creation of German knights, monks and settlers who at that time had moved into those eastern territories. Not only were their descendants now driven back to the west: but the descendants also of the Western Slav peoples whom they originally found there and with whom they had long been inextricably mixed. This is not historical justice. It was an atrocity, the final atrocity of a war which had more than its share in atrocities, admittedly begun by Germany under Hitler; and as to the atrocities, it was the Germans, unfortunately, who had initiated them too.

What does one do about atrocities, how does one cope with them? Keeping a score is no use; thoughts of revenge only make everything worse. Someone has to find the magnanimity to say: 'This is enough.' To have been able to do that is a title to glory that no one can take from the expelled Prussians. Anyone so disposed may call the matter-of-fact way in which they, without any thought of revenge, and soon without any thought of return, have made themselves at home and useful in Western Germany evidence of Prussian matter-of-factness. It lends to the sad story of Prussia's slow demise something of a ringing final chord.

MAPS

Brandenburg-Prussia from 1415 to 1918

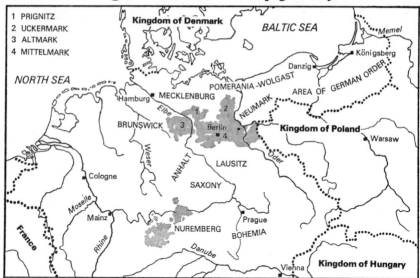

1415-1440: Frederick, Sixth Burgrave of Nuremberg, receives the Mark Brandenburg (dark grey) from King Sigismund in 1415. On the death of this first Elector of Brandenburg the country, together with Ansbach and Bayreuth, covered an area of 29,478 sq. km.

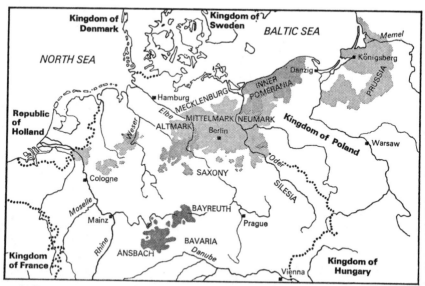

1640-1688: By the time of the accession of the Elector Frederick Wilhelm Brandenburg-Prussia had more than doubled in size. It now also acquired colonies on the Gold Coast and in the West Indies and, on the death of the Great Elector, covered an area of 110,836 sq. km.

inherited territory   acquired or conquered territory

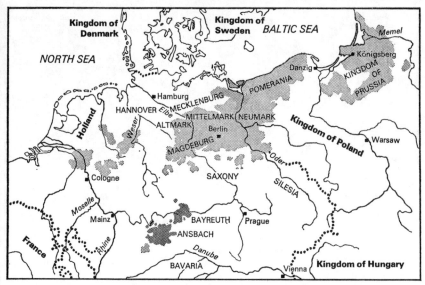

1688-1740: In 1701 the Elector Frederick III became King Frederick I in Prussia. He left his son a territory only slightly larger than the one he inherited. In 1740, on the death of Frederick Wilhelm I, the state, together with Orange and Neuchatel, covered an area of 118,926 sq. km.

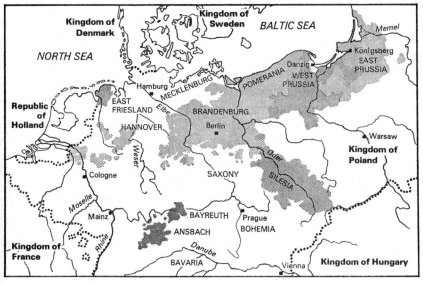

1740-1786: Under Frederick the Great Prussia grew considerably (mid-grey); among others, Silesia, West Prussia and the Netze district were added. He left his successor a country of 5,430,000 inhabitants and an area of 194,891 sq. km.

▨ possessions of the colateral line

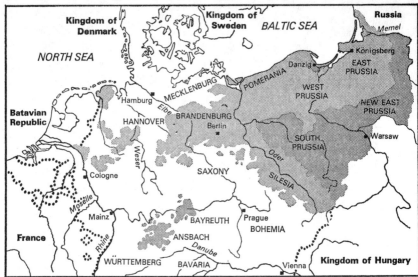

1786-1797: During the short reign of Frederick Wilhelm II the state attained its hitherto greatest extent: 305,659 sq. km. (the Federal Republic of Germany covers 247,975 sq. km.). The increase was due to the territories which Poland lost to Prussia in 1792 and 1795.

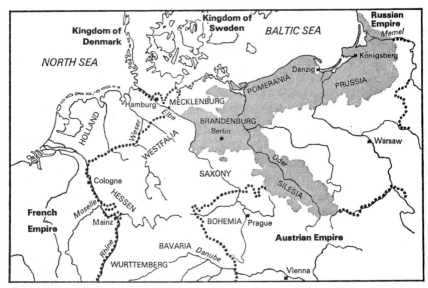

1807-1815: By the Peace of Tilsit Prussia had to surrender half its territory, including all lands west of the Elbe, the major part of the Netze area and the Polish acquisitions. The territories remaining Prussian are tinted light grey.

inherited territory   acquired or conquered territory

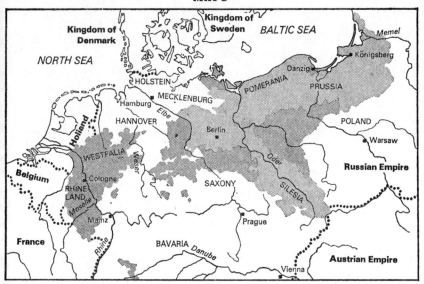

1815-1861: The Congress of Vienna (1814-15) reordered Europe. Prussia, in addition to what it possessed prior to 1807, received parts of Saxony, Westphalia and the territory on the left bank of the Rhine. 1815: 10,400,000 inhabitants, 278,042 sq. km.; 1861: 19,600,000 inhabitants.

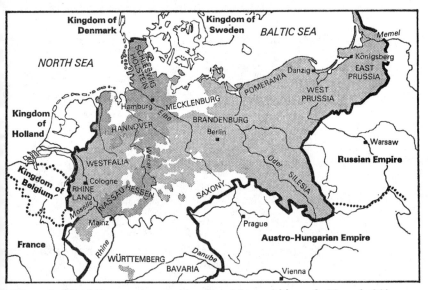

1861-1918: The dark grey area comprises Prussia's acquisitions of 1864 and 1866, the Duchy of Lauenberg was not incorporated until 1876. In 1871 Wilhelm I became Emperor of the German Reich whose frontiers are marked by the heavy black line.

CHRONOLOGICAL TABLE

1134   Margrave Albrecht the Bear enfeoffed with the Northern Mark Brandenburg.

1226   The Golden Bull of Rimini authorizes the Order of the Teutonic Knights to rule the territory of the *Pruzzen*.

1320   End of the Ascanian dynasty in Brandenburg.

1415   Frederick, Sixth Burgrave of Nuremberg, becomes Frederick I, Margrave of Brandenburg; b. 6.8.1371, d. 21.9.1440.

1440   Frederick II, b. 19.11.1413, d. 10.2.1471, Elector of Brandenburg.

1466   By the Second Peace of Thorn the Grand Master of the Teutonic Order is compelled to swear fealty to Poland.

1470   Albrecht Achilles, b. 24.11.1414, d. 11.3.1486, Elector of B.

1486   Johann Cicero, b. 2.8.1455, d. 9.1.1499, Elector of B.

1499   Joachim I Nestor, b. 21.2.1484, d. 11.7.1535, Elector of B.

1511   Albrecht von Brandenburg-Ansbach becomes Grand Master of the Teutonic Order.

1525   The Teutonic Order state is transformed into the temporal Duchy of Prussia.

1535   Joachim II Hector, b. 9.1.1505, d. 3.1.1571, Elector of B.

1539   Reformation in Brandenburg through Elector Joachim II Hector.

1544   Foundation of University of Königsberg.

1571   Johann Georg, b. 11.4.1525, d. 8.1.1598, Elector of B.

1598   Joachim Frederick, b. 27.1.1546, d. 18.7.1608, Elector of B.

1608   Johann Sigismund, b. 8.11.1572, d. 23.12.1619, Elector of B.

1618 Elector Johann Sigismund is acknowledged as Duke of Prussia.
Start of Thirty Years' War.

1619 Georg Wilhelm, b. 3.11.1595, d. 1.12.1640, Elector of B.

1640 Frederick Wilhelm, b. 6.2.1620, d. 29.4.1688, Elector of B. (the Great Elector).

1648 Peace Treaty of Westphalia: Brandenburg receives Eastern Pomerania.

1660 Peace of Oliva: Prussia becomes a sovereign state.

1675 The Great Elector defeats the Swedes at Fehrbellin.

1685 Edict of Potsdam: the Huguenots are received in Brandenburg.

1686 Frederick III, b. 11.7.1657, d. 25.2.1713, Elector of B. Third son of Frederick Wilhelm by marriage with Luise Henriette (1627–67), daughter of Prince Henry of Nassau-Orange. Married (1) 1679 Elisabeth Henriette of Hesse-Kassel (1661–83); (2) 1684 Sophie Charlotte (1668–1705), daughter of the Elector Ernst August of Hanover; (3) 1708 Sophie Luise of Mecklenburg-Schwerin (1685–1735). One child from first marriage, two children from second marriage.

1698 'Old man Dessau', Leopold von Anhalt-Dessau, introduces marching in step in the Prussian Army.
Andreas Schlüter begins construction of the Berlin Palace and the equestrian statue of the Great Elector.

1700 Gottfried Wilhelm von Leibniz founds the Prussian Academy of Sciences in Berlin and becomes its President.

1701 The Sovereign Duchy of Prussia becomes a Kingdom. Elector Frederick III becomes King Frederick I in Prussia.

1704 The *Berlinische Nachrichten von Staats- und Gelehrten Sachen* appears in Berlin, the precursor of the *Vossische Zeitung*.

1710 The Charité Hospital is founded in Berlin.

1713 Frederick Wilhelm I, b. 14.8.1688, d. 31.5.1740, King in P. Second son of Frederick I by second marriage. Married 1706 Sophie Dorothea (1687–1757), daughter of King George I of England, fourteen children.

By the Peace of Utrecht Prussia is recognized as a Kingdom. Johann Friedrich von Eosander, called von Göthe, supervises the extension of the Berlin Palace.

1714   Prussia abolishes witch trials, following the demand for their abolition in Christian Thomasius's pamphlet 'De crimine magiae'.

1715   Prussia joins the Nordic War and conquers Western Pomerania and Stralsund.

1717   General compulsory education introduced in Prussia.

1720   The Nordic war (which started in 1700) ends and Prussia, by the Peace of Stockholm, receives Stettin, Western Pomerania as far as Usedom, and Wollin as far as the Peene.

Johann Sebastian Bach composes his 'Brandenburg Concertos'.

1723   A General Directorate is set up in Prussia as the supreme administrative authority.

1730   Prince Frederick's attempt to escape is prevented and he and his accomplice Lt. von Katte are arrested. Frederick is punished by imprisonment, his friend Katte is executed.

1731–   Resettlement of East Prussia following its depopulation
32   by the plague. Frederick Wilhelm I settles over 20,000 Protestants, expelled from Salzburg, in those territories.

1739   Voltaire publishes the *Anti-Machiavelli* written by Frederick (II), a plea for moral government.

1740   Frederick II, b. 24.1.1712, d. 17.8.1786, King in P. (third son of Frederick Wilhelm I). Married 1733 Elisabeth (1715–97) daughter of Duke Ferdinand Albrecht II of Braunschweig-Wolfenbüttel; marriage childless.

Beginning of the Austrian War of Succession (until 1748) and of the First Silesian War (1740–42).

Torture abolished in Prussia. Frederick II establishes religious toleration.

The Order 'Pour le Mérite' is introduced in Prussia.

1742   In the Peace of Breslau Prussia receives Upper and Lower Silesia and the county of Glatz.

The Elbe-Havel Canal is constructed.

1743   The Berlin Opera House (architect: Knobelsdorff) is completed.

1744   Outbreak of Second Silesian War.
A cotton manufactory is set up in Berlin.
Knobelsdorff starts construction of Sanssouci Castle.

1745   By the Peace of Dresden Austria confirms Prussia in the possession of Silesia and Frederick recognizes Maria Theresa's husband, Francis I, as Emperor.

1746   Frederick II writes (in French) the *History of My Age*.

1750   A porcelain manufactory is founded in Berlin.
Voltaire visits Frederick II at Sanssouci and stays for three years.

1756   Outbreak of Seven Years' War. In this war Prussia fights against the Great Coalition of Austria, France, Russia, Sweden and the Empire.
Moses Mendelssohn in Prussia supports the emancipation of the Jews. Lessing works as reviewer on the *Vossische Zeitung*.

1760   Berlin occupied by Russian troops for the first time.

1762   The Empress Elizabeth of Russia dies and Peter III enters into alliance with Frederick II.

1763   In the Peace of Hubertusburg Prussia's possession of Silesia is confirmed. Prussia becomes a great power.
General Education Act in Prussia introduces compulsory schooling between the ages of five and thirteen.

1770   Kant becomes Professor at Königsberg.

1772   First partition of Poland: Prussia receives West Prussia (less Danzig and Thorn), Ermland and the Netze district.

1774   Johann Gottfried Herder publishes his *Philosophy of the History of the Education of Mankind*.

1781   Kant writes his *Critique of Pure Reason*.

1786   Frederick Wilhelm II, b. 25.9.1744, d. 16.11.1797, King of P. First son of August Wilhelm (a brother of Frederick II) and Luise, daughter of Duke Ferdinand Albrecht II of Braunschweig-Wolfenbüttel. Married (1) 1765 Elisabeth of Braunschweig-Wolfenbüttel (1746–1840, divorced

1769); (2) 1769 Friedrike (1751–1805), daughter of Landgrave Ludwig IX of Hesse-Darmstadt. One child from first marriage, eight children from second marriage. Two further morganatic marriages. Issue of that with Sophie Countess Döhnhoff became the Counts of Brandenburg; five children were born to his mistress Wilhelmine Enke (Countess Lichtenau).

1788 Kant publishes his second principal work, the *Critique of Practical Reason*.

1789 In the year of the French Revolution Carl Gotthardt Langhans builds the Brandenburg Gate.

1792 First Coalition War (1792–97): France against Austria and Prussia; cannonade of Valmy, which ends undecisively.

Foundation of the Berlin Academy of Singing.

1793 Second partition of Poland: Prussia receives Posen and Kalisch, Danzig and Thorn.

1794 The Prussian General Code of Law, created by Carl Gottlieb Svarez, comes into effect.

Johann Gottfried Schadow completes the quadriga on top of the Brandenburg Gate.

1795 Third partition of Poland between Prussia, Austria and Russia. Prussia takes Mazovia, Warsaw and the territory between the rivers Vistula, Bug and Niemen.

1797 Frederick Wilhelm III, b. 3.8.1770, d. 7.6.1840, King of P. First son by second marriage of Frederick Wilhelm II. Married (1) 1793 Luise (1776–1810), daughter of Duke Karl II of Mecklenburg-Strelitz; (2) 1824 Auguste, Princess of Liegnitz (1800–73); nine children from first marriage.

Kant writes his *Metaphysics of Custom*.

August Wilhelm von Schlegel starts on his translations of Shakespeare.

Ludwig Tieck writes his *Popular Fairy Tales*.

1799 In the Second Coalition War (1799–1802) against France Prussia remains neutral.

Alexander von Humboldt makes an exploratory journey to Central and South America.

Friedrich Schleiermacher writes *On Religion*.

1806   With the exception of Austria, Prussia, Kurhessen and Braunschweig all German states join Napoleon's 'Confederation of the Rhine'. Outbreak of war between France on the one side and Prussia and Russia on the other.

1807   In the Peace of Tilsit Prussia loses all its territories west of the Elbe and hence about half its area and population. Freiherr von Stein introduces liberal reforms (emancipation of the peasantry, urban administration, civil service reform).

1808   Carl von Clausewitz, Gerhard von Scharnhorst and August Neithardt von Gneisenau embark on the reform of the Prussian Army.

Johann Gottlieb Fichte delivers his 'Speeches to the German Nation' in Berlin.

1809   Wilhelm von Humboldt becomes Prussian Minister of Education.

1810   Karl August Prince of Hardenberg continues the reforms in Prussia following Stein's dismissal.

Freedom of trade proclaimed in Prussia.

Heinrich von Kleist writes *Prince Frederick of Homburg*.

1812   General Yorck von Wartenburg on his own authority concludes a neutrality agreement with the Russians. This marks the beginning of the Wars of Liberation.

Friedrich Ludwig Jahn sets up the first gymnastics field in Berlin.

1813   In the Battle of the Nations at Leipzig Napoleon is crushingly defeated by the combined Prussians, Austrians, and Russians, and forced to retreat beyond the Rhine.

1814   The Allies occupy Paris and Napoleon is deposed.

The Congress of Vienna opens.

E.T.A. Hoffmann publishes his *Fantastic Pieces*.

1815   Napoleon returns from banishment but is defeated at Waterloo by Blücher and Wellington and forced finally to abdicate.

Rahel Varnhagen continues to conduct her intellectual salon.

August Wilhelm Iffland dies. He was the first to make the Berlin theatre famous.

Following Europe's reorganization by the Congress of Vienna Russia, Prussia and Austria form the 'Holy Alliance' against liberal and revolutionary movements.

1819 The Karlsbad decrees introduce press censorship, banning of students' organizations, supervision of universities and teachers. Beginning of the persecution of 'demagogues'; Arndt and Schleiermacher are relieved of their offices, Jahn is arrested.

1821 First performance of Carl Maria von Weber's opera *Der Freischütz* at Schinkel's new theatre in the Gendarmenmarkt.

1826 Felix Mendelssohn-Bartholdy writes the overture to *A Midsummer Night's Dream.*

1833 The German Customs Union is founded, comprising eighteen German states.

Ban on the liberal books of the 'Young Germany' movement.

1837 August Borsig sets up an iron foundry and an engineering establishment in Berlin.

1838– The first Prussian railway runs between Berlin and
39 Potsdam.

To improve fitness for military service child labour in factories is prohibited in Prussia for children under nine.

1840 Frederick Wilhelm IV, b. 15.10.1795, d. 2.1.1861, King of P. First son by first marriage of Frederick Wilhelm III. Married 1823 Elisabeth of Bavaria (1801–73). Marriage childless.

1842 Frederick Wilhelm IV lays the foundation stone for the completion of Cologne Cathedral.

Karl Marx works as editor of the *Rheinische Zeitung* in Cologne before being compelled to emigrate to Paris in 1843.

1844 The weavers' risings in Silesia are ruthlessly crushed.

1845 Alexander von Humboldt publishes his five-volume work *Cosmos, a Draft of a Physical Description of the World.*

1847 Frederick Wilhelm IV summons the eight provincial Diets to Berlin as a 'United Diet of the Monarchy'.

1848 Revolutionary fighting in Prussia (March revolution).

Otto von Bismarck founds the conservative *Neue Preussische Zeitung (Kreuzzeitung)* in Berlin.

Kladderadatsch appears as a political satirical journal.

1849 Frederick Wilhelm IV declines the imperial crown; Prussia is given an 'imposed' constitution.

Prussia establishes the Union of German Princes (twenty-eight states).

1850 Under the Treaty of Olmütz the 'German Confederation' is restored and the 'German Union' is dissolved.

Austria maintains its predominant position in Germany.

1851 Otto von Bismarck becomes Prussia's Minister to the German Bundestag.

1854 Jakob and Wilhelm Grimm start work on their *German Dictionary.*

1857 Frederick Wilhelm IV renounces his rights to Neuchâtel. Wilhelm (I) assumes the regency for his brother Frederick Wilhelm IV.

1858 Rudolf Virchow lays the foundations of cellular pathology.

1861 Wilhelm I, b. 22.3.1787, d. 9.3.1889, King of P., brother of Frederick Wilhelm IV. Married 1829 Auguste (1811–1890) daughter of Grand Duke Karl Frederick of Saxe-Weimar. Two children.

1862 Dissolution of the Prussian Assembly following a constitutional quarrel from the preceding year about the strengthening of the army by War Minister Albrecht von Roon. Otto von Bismarck becomes Prussian Minister President.

1864 Prussian-Austrian war against Denmark.

1866 Prussia's war against Austria for predominance in Germany.

1867 Bismarck becomes Chancellor of the North German Confederation founded by him.

1869 Foundation of the Social Democrat Workers' Party.

1870– War of the North German Confederation and the South
71 German states against France.

1871 Foundation of the German Empire. Wilhelm I becomes German Emperor, Bismarck becomes Reich Chancellor.

1872 Bismarck's *Kulturkampf* against the Catholic Centre Party begins in Prussia.
In Prussia the state assumes supervision of the schools.

1878 Bismarck causes the 'socialist laws' to be passed for the suppression of the working-class movement.

1879 Werner von Siemens builds the first electric locomotive.

1882 Robert Koch, founder of bacteriology, discovers the tuberculosis bacillus.
Theodor Fontane completes his '*Rambles through the Mark Brandenburg*'.

1883 Bismarck embarks on his social legislation.

1887 Bismarck concludes a secret reinsurance treaty with Russia.

1888 Frederick III Wilhelm, b. 18.5.1831, d. 15.6.1888, German Emperor, King of P., first son of Wilhelm I. Married 1858 Victoria of Great Britain (1840–1901), daughter of Prince Albert of Saxe-Coburg-Gotha and Queen Victoria. Eight children.
Wilhelm II, b. 27.1.1859, d. 4.6.1941, German Emperor, King of P., first son of Frederick III. Married (1) 1881 Auguste Viktoria of Schleswig-Holstein (1858–1921); (2) 1922 Hermine von Reuss. Seven children by first marriage.

1889 Major strikes break out in the Ruhr.
Gerhart Hauptmann writes *Before Dawn*.
Otto Brahm founds the 'Free Theatre' in Berlin.

1890 Bismarck dismissed by Wilhelm II.

1893 Emil von Behring develops the diphtheria serum.

1897 Alfred von Tirpitz on Wilhelm II's instruction devotes himself to building up the German Navy.

1898 Max Liebermann founds the Berlin *Sezession*.
Alfred Messel starts construction of the Wertheim Department Store, thereby decisively influencing the subsequent 'new realism' in architecture.

1905   Wilhelm II triggers off the first Moroccan crisis.

Max Reinhardt takes over the German Theatre in Berlin.

1908   Wilhelm II gives an interview to the *Daily Telegraph* and is sharply criticized at home and abroad.

1911   Second Moroccan crisis resulting from the despatch of the German gunboat *Panther*.

1912   The Social Democrats become the strongest party in the Reichstag.

1914   Power policy conflicts in Europe lead to the First World War.

1916   Hindenburg becomes Chief of the Supreme Army Command Staff.

1917   Wilhelm II promises the introduction of secret direct suffrage in Prussia.

George Grosz produces his volume of lithographs *The Face of the Ruling Class*.

1918   Prince Max of Baden becomes German Reich Chancellor and on his own responsibility announces Kaiser Wilhelm II's abdication.

Karl Liebknecht proclaims a Republic of Councils.

Philipp Scheidemann proclaims the Republic.

1919   Friedrich Ebert becomes the first German Reich President. The constituent Prussian Assembly proposes a unified German state; Konrad Adenauer, Lord Mayor of Cologne, proposes separation of the Rhineland from Prussia.

1920   Otto Braun becomes Prussian Minister President, Carl Severing becomes Prussian Minister of the Interior.

Max Liebermann becomes President of the Prussian Academy of Arts.

1921   Konrad Adenauer becomes President of the Prussian State Council.

1925   Following Friedrich Ebert's death Paul von Hindenburg is elected Reich President.

Foundation of the Berlin Architects' Association 'Ring' (Mies van der Rohe, Gropius, May, Bartning, Mendelsohn).

1927   Heinrich Zille publishes 'The Big Zille Album'.

1928 Bertolt Brecht's and Kurt Weill's *The Threepenny Opera* has its first performance in Berlin and achieves worldwide success.

1932 In the Prussian Diet elections the gains of the National Socialists shake the Social Democrat Government of Braun and Severing. Hindenburg is re-elected Reich President.
Coup d'état by Franz von Papen. The Braun-Severing Government is deposed; von Papen assumes Prussian state business as Reich Commissar for Prussia.

1933 Hindenburg appoints Adolf Hitler Reich Chancellor. The last remnants of Prussian state independence surviving in the Weimar Republic are liquidated.

1937 Gustaf Gründgens becomes Controller General of the Prussian State Theatres in Berlin.

1939 Germany occupies the Memel territory, Hitler demands Danzig and a corridor to West Prussia.
Outbreak of the Second World War.

1944 German officers make an attempt on the life of Adolf Hitler.

1945 Conquest of Prussia's eastern territories by the Russians triggers off a mass flight.
The Potsdam Conference decides in favour of the 'resettlement' of the remaining population.

1947 The state of Prussia is declared abolished by Allied Control Council Law of 25 February.

INDEX